*More praise for*

# The Unmaking
# of the
# President 2016

"Anyone who cares about understanding the most startling election in U.S. history must confront the analysis and evidence so skillfully deployed by Lanny Davis. Whether you're a Trump True Believer or a Hillary Diehard, you'll never come to terms with the amazements and outrages of the 2016 campaign until you've confronted this indispensable book. Many readers will disagree with some of its explosive conclusions (as I did), but no one can disregard all of them."

—Michael Medved, nationally syndicated conservative
talk show host, bestselling author, and member of
the Board of Contributors for *USA Today*

"Lanny Davis details the full, horrifying story of how one man's decisions to violate policy and common sense helped to upend an election and, as a consequence, change the course of American history. One of our keenest political observers, Davis lays out a meticulous case against James Comey, the former director of the FBI, whose repeated and unprecedented interference in the 2016 election transformed what is supposed to be a politically silent government post into that of a virtual third candidate. . . . Davis's book is at once disturbing, fascinating, and informative. It is a must-read for anyone who cares about the future of democracy."

—Kurt Eichenwald, contributing editor at
*Vanity Fair* and bestselling author

"Everybody wants to know how Hillary Clinton lost the election to Donald Trump. Lanny Davis has the answer, and it's indisputable: the blame lies squarely on then–FBI director James Comey and his ill-considered, ill-fated, and lethal letter of October 28. Lanny Davis and Donald Trump agree on one thing: James Comey should have been fired. The difference, as Davis proves conclusively, is that Comey should have been fired by President Obama for violating rules of the Justice Department, interfering in a presidential election, and throwing the election to Donald Trump."

—Bill Press, former moderator of CNN's *Crossfire*,
nationally syndicated columnist, and progressive
Democrat TV/radio talk show host

## ALSO BY LANNY J. DAVIS

*Crisis Tales: Five Rules for Coping with Crises in Business, Politics, and Life*

*Scandal: How "Gotcha" Politics Is Destroying America*

*Truth to Tell: Tell It Early, Tell It All, Tell It Yourself:*
*Notes from My White House Education*

# The Unmaking
## of the
# President 2016

How FBI Director James Comey
Cost Hillary Clinton the Presidency

# Lanny J. Davis

SCRIBNER
New York  London  Toronto  Sydney  New Delhi

Scribner
An Imprint of Simon & Schuster, Inc.
1230 Avenue of the Americas
New York, NY 10020

First Scribner trade paperback edition September 2018

SCRIBNER and design are registered trademarks of The Gale Group, Inc.,
used under license by Simon & Schuster, Inc., the publisher of this work.

For information about special discounts for bulk purchases,
please contact Simon & Schuster Special Sales at 1-866-506-1949
or business@simonandschuster.com.

The Simon & Schuster Speakers Bureau can bring authors to
your live event. For more information or to book an event, contact the
Simon & Schuster Speakers Bureau at 1-866-248-3049 or
visit our website at www.simonspeakers.com.

Interior design by Kyle Kabel

Manufactured in the United States of America

3   5   7   9   10   8   6   4   2

Library of Congress Cataloging-in-Publication Data has been applied for.

ISBN 978-1-5011-7772-9
ISBN 978-1-5011-8039-2 (pbk)
ISBN 978-1-5011-8040-8 (ebook)

To Carolyn Atwell-Davis
wife, partner, friend, critic,
always there through thick and thin

Imagine how history would judge today's Americans if, looking back at this election, the record showed that voters empowered a dangerous man because of . . . a minor email scandal. There is no equivalence between Ms. Clinton's wrongs and Mr. Trump's manifest unfitness for office.

—*Washington Post*, editorial,
September 8, 2016

[Impeachable offenses] proceed from the misconduct of public men, or, in other words, from the abuse or violation of some public trust. They are of a nature which may . . . be denominated political, as they relate chiefly to injuries done immediately to the society itself.

—Alexander Hamilton,
Federalist Papers, No. 65,
March 7, 1788

# Contents

# The Illegitimate President

Hillary Clinton lost the 2016 presidential election and Donald Trump won it for the single, decisive reason that FBI director James Comey wrote his infamous letter to Congress on October 28, 2016, announcing the discovery of a laptop computer belonging to Anthony Weiner that contained thousands of copies of Clinton's emails. This strange and surprising news mere days before the election eroded Clinton's support just enough that she lost the electoral college despite handily winning the popular vote. Some reasonable people continue to disagree with this assertion, citing Clinton's campaign flaws or Trump's appeal to his base of voters. But although such explanations may make the election results more logical, or less absurd, they are essentially wrong. All available pre– vs. post–October 28 election poll data indicates that Hillary Clinton would have won the election had Comey not sent the letter.

Indeed, the assertion that Comey's letter cost Clinton the election has become more widely accepted, especially—ironically—after Comey was fired by Trump. Yet the letter was the final event in a sequence that will only gain historical importance and scrutiny in the years ahead. Today, as the Trump administration lurches from one self-created crisis to the next, it is important to more fully understand the events—many widely known but others comprehended by only a few—that led to this unexpected outcome, an election so bizarre and cataclysmic in its nature and magnitude that next to the 9/11 attacks, it stands as the most important event in America in the twenty-first century to date. History and truth require a full accounting. That is the intention of this book.

But there also is a more timely context to this book, which was completed in October 2017. Between May 9, 2017, when Trump fired Comey over his refusal to halt the Russia-collusion investigation, and June 8, when Comey accused Trump of trying to impede his investigation, there was a serious possibility of an impeachment investigation based on an attempted obstruction of justice and for other reasons. At the time of this writing, Trump's unpredictable and offensive behavior has furthered the call for his removal, potentially under the Twenty-Fifth Amendment for mental impairment that puts the nation at risk. Thus it is now exponentially more important to show that Trump became president only because Comey wrote his letter. Add to this the insidious influence of the Russians in spreading fake news about Clinton with evidence that Trump campaign officials or associates communicated with Russian officials during the campaign. If an impeachment investigation process begins, the fact that Trump was elected by illegitimate means is the best rebuttal to those who would oppose the investigation in the belief that it was an unimpaired free and fair election. The election *was* impaired—by James Comey—and the stakes for America's future could not be higher.

# PART I

# The Invention
# of a Scandal

# CHAPTER ONE

# The Wary Candidate

Any discussion of why Hillary Clinton decided to use a private server for her emails and why the revelation of that fact contributed to her 2016 Election Day loss must begin with a political truth about her: Despite the millions of voters who revere her, she has long been the target of hatred, criticism, and misinformation. In her more than thirty-five years of public life—beginning as the spouse of a six-term governor in 1978, her experience as first lady in the White House over two terms of Bill Clinton's presidency, then as a senator from New York, as a presidential candidate in 2008, and as secretary of state before her 2016 campaign—she has learned to be cautious when dealing with the media.

No one in public political life, especially Hillary Clinton, would claim that tough treatment by the media doesn't go with the territory. There has been legitimate criticism that Clinton and her 2016 campaign staff were not sufficiently prepared to deal with the emails story. But one way to understand her behavior is to put it in the context of what she had learned years earlier in dealing with a generally critical media.

There are many episodes from Clinton's public life that offer insight into her and her campaign's initial instincts in dealing with the email server story, but several stand out.

Perhaps the most dramatic was the invented scandal called

Whitewater. When the *New York Times* broke the story on its front page on March 8, 1992, most readers had a hard time figuring out what the scandal was, much less understanding a very confusing story. Even the headline was odd, since it didn't seem to merit front-page treatment—"THE 1992 CAMPAIGN: Personal Finances; Clintons Joined S.&L. Operator in an Ozark Real-Estate Venture."

It was also inaccurate. The partner of the Clintons referred to, James McDougal, was not an S&L operator in 1978, when they made a real estate investment with him and his wife, Susan (he became an S&L operator only years later). In any case, the entire story was as simple as this: Mr. and Mrs. McDougal approached the Clintons in 1978 about purchasing about two hundred acres of land in the picturesque Ozark Mountains in northwest Arkansas, alongside the White River, to subdivide the land and build and sell vacation homes. Hillary Clinton took the lead in paperwork, financial decisions, and trying to keep up with the details.

Just as the Clintons and McDougals together borrowed $200,000 for what was called the Whitewater Development Corporation, interest rates hit 20 percent and the vacation-home-buying market dried up. Their investment failed. Years later, the only offense ever shown by Hillary and Bill Clinton regarding their Whitewater activities was their taking a $4,000 personal tax deduction for interest instead of a deduction for their corporation. They ended up repaying the IRS, plus interest, for the value of that deduction.

That was the entire Whitewater story—and it didn't change very much over the years. But because it was a front-page story in the *Times*, a lot of journalists, as is their custom, figured there must be more there than met the eye. And off they went. The sordid details of all the other branches and sub-branches of the bogus "scandal" called Whitewater are not relevant here. But reading over the headlines in the 1990s involving Whitewater, often on the front pages of the nation's three major newspapers—the *New York Times*, the *Washington*

*Post*, and the *Wall Street Journal*—as well as the breathless reporting every night on the major TV news programs—leaves even an objective observer with the inevitable takeaway: What was that all about? Where was the beef?

And through it all, Hillary Clinton received most of the blame, especially for putting her apparently uninvolved husband at great risk, even imperiling his presidency. But blame for what? After seven years of investigation by Republicans in Congress and two independent counsels, $60 million of taxpayer funds, thousands of inflammatory headlines, Senate and House televised hearings and investigations, including a Senate special committee on Whitewater, which involved 300 hours of hearings and more than 60 sessions over 13 months and 10,000 pages of testimony and 35,000 pages of depositions from almost 250 people—at the end of the day, what was the verdict on Bill and Hillary Clinton and Whitewater?

Nothing. The final report of the last independent counsel, Robert Ray (who succeeded Kenneth Starr), in 2000, stated that there was "insufficient evidence" to bring any charges against Bill or Hillary Clinton regarding Whitewater.

So what lessons did Hillary Clinton learn during Whitewater about dealing with a mainstream media driven by or acting in parallel with a right-wing Republican complex feeding on and reinforcing each other? Two important moments stand out about how to handle the media when the facts get lost in the hurricane-force winds of reporters smelling controversy and scandal, even when there are no facts to support any charge of illegal conduct.

First, on April 22, 1994, after Hillary Clinton became the focal point of media interest and innuendo about "wrongdoing" in Whitewater, she took the advice of all her political and media advisers to follow the classic crisis management strategy: Get out in front and be 100 percent accessible and answer all questions. She sat in an armchair under a portrait of Abraham Lincoln in the State Dining Room of the White House. For more than an hour, on live television, wearing a pink jacket (and thus known thereafter as the "pink press conference"), she answered all questions—constructive, mean-spirited, and everything in between. Facts, facts, facts. That is all she did.

In May 2015, twenty-one years later, *Time* magazine's Michael Duffy wrote a piece recalling the pink press conference. Duffy was no easy reporter when it came to coverage of the Clintons—far from it. But this is what he remembered, and it was accurate, reflecting the reactions of everyone who watched her on live TV and most of the gathered White House press corps: "What happened was a riveting hour and 12 minutes in which the First Lady appeared to be open, candid, but above all unflappable. While she provided little new information on the tangled Arkansas land deal or her controversial commodity trades, the real message was her attitude and her poise. The confiding tone and relaxed body language, which was seen live on four networks, immediately drew approving reviews."

(The same could be said for Secretary of State Clinton's appearance—for eleven hours!—before Rep. Trey Gowdy's Select Committee on Benghazi on October 22, 2015. She won the day and got the same rave reviews for her poise and focus on the facts under grilling by the sometimes frantic Gowdy and his fellow frustrated, partisan Republican colleagues.)

So during Whitewater she took the political crisis management advice and thought she had succeeded. And what happened? Nothing. That's right, nothing changed. Indeed, the coverage on Whitewater and the focus on her as the evildoer and potential criminal cover-up artist got worse. It got so bad that, two years later, for the first time in U.S. history, a first lady was called before a grand jury to testify. Not only called but in fact forced by what seemed to be an overzealous group of Whitewater prosecutors to do the public "perp walk" that prosecutors like to put prominent Wall Street investment bankers through when they are arrested and handcuffed, with TV cameras and the media prompted to come and record the walk for ultimate humiliation. It didn't matter that Hillary Clinton was the nation's first lady, and she should have been given greater courtesy, if only out of respect for the office of the presidency.

So perhaps it was logical for her to conclude that no matter how she "handled" a controversial media story about anything she did, including admitting an honest mistake, once there was any hint of "scandal," however unfounded, perhaps feeding the "beast" of the media horde would only make matters worse.

Then came her 2007–2008 presidential campaign. It was expected that as the front-runner and overwhelming consensus candidate to win the Democratic nomination and then the presidency, Clinton would be the target of the toughest and most critical media coverage. But in this instance, the piling on of any Hillary Clinton mistake was so egregious, so obviously a gang-up by both the media and all the other candidates, especially during the televised debates, that it was beyond anything experienced by other (male) front-runners.

Now she encountered a few Clinton critics among certain journalists and columnists who were generally considered "liberal" but whose venom and hatred toward Bill and Hillary bordered on the pathological. The one who took first place in this category by a large margin was the *New York Times* columnist Maureen Dowd. Her anti-Hillary rants and personal attacks on Clinton sometimes suggested she was bitter and angry out of sheer envy. And then there was the unforgettable moment in 2007 that defined what Clinton was up against when Chris Matthews, an extremely bright and politically savvy TV commentator for MSNBC, lost any semblance of political balance in his comments about Barack Obama after a particularly compelling speech at a key moment of the presidential nomination battle. On Super Tuesday, March 28, 2008, in which Obama had fought Clinton to a virtual tie among the states that had voted, Matthews described

Obama's televised speech as "the best speech I've ever heard . . . and I'm tearing up . . ." Then he compared Obama—I am not making this up—to Jesus, or close to it: "I've been following politics since I was about five," he said. "I've never seen anything like this. This is bigger than Kennedy. [Obama] comes along, and he seems to have the answers. This is the New Testament."

And if that wasn't over the top enough, Matthews went even further, apparently without embarrassment: "I have to tell you, you know, it's part of reporting this case, this election, the feeling most people get when they hear Barack Obama's speech. I felt this thrill going up my leg."

That thrill-going-up-my-leg moment—and not to blame Matthews, whose emotional and political attraction to the truly inspirational Barack Obama was genuine—was a symbol of what Hillary Clinton had grown accustomed to from those covering the campaign. If she made a simple slip or error, everyone jumped all over her, virtually the entire press corps, talking heads, and most political reporters. But when it came to judging her compared to Barack Obama, the effort was hopeless—although it must be said that in Obama, she was running against an orator and inspirational figure who was truly the political phenomenon of our time.

But it's hard to imagine any human not becoming somewhat defensive and restrained in the face of such a combination of intense media hostility and the magical positive media that Barack Obama so often received (and deservedly so) during that campaign.

So from her days as spouse of a governor, to her days as first lady, to her days as a presidential candidate in 2008, and all the days in between, Hillary Clinton knew that she was always going to be the object of negative media because that is the way it was, and she had better get used to it. The only two exceptions to that rule were when she served in the Senate, where she was one of the most popular Democratic senators—among Republican as well as Democratic colleagues (West Virginia Democratic senator Robert Byrd referred to her as "a workhorse, not a show horse"); and when she served as Obama's secretary of state, when her popularity ratings soared into the 60s and 70s, with relatively high approval ratings even among grassroots Republicans. In both of these jobs, hard work and facts were more important than perceptions and caricatures created by a cynical media, fed by partisan right-wing haters.

So this is the life experience in public service that shaped Hillary Clinton's judgment of how to handle a negative press story that had the potential to spread into scandal mania: Be cautious and assume that "feeding the beast" might turn what would otherwise be a passing controversy into a negative story that never goes away.

With all this in mind, we turn to the question of Clinton's emails while she was secretary of state. The story begins with a plain fact: Hillary Clinton loved her BlackBerry.

She used it to stay in touch with the thousands of friends to whom she had remained close since grade school, high school, college, law school, and all the public service and political years as first lady of Arkansas and of the United States, and as a senator. Her friends grew accustomed to shooting her quick personal notes, passing along jokes, and commenting on serious issues, receiving amazingly prompt and often funny or interesting or erudite responses, often within a matter of minutes or hours, no matter how busy she was.

There may have been an evening in December 2008 or January 2009, after Hillary Clinton had been named by President-elect Barack Obama to be his secretary of state, that she and some senior aides discussed whether it mattered if she used one BlackBerry as she always had to communicate with her friends while also communicating as secretary of state, or whether she needed to carry one for personal messages and another for official State Department business. Like almost every other member of Congress, she had come to rely for convenience on a single BlackBerry rather than two.

She was well aware that everything she did would be leaked if her right-wing adversaries and haters had a chance; even her most personal and private messages would appear not just on the front pages of tabloids but maybe also on the front page of the *New York Times*. Thus she decided to use a private email address and her husband's private server at their home in Chappaqua, New York. It was physically protected by the former president's ongoing Secret Service detail and had been established with multiple security systems to prevent hacking. She knew that all of her official business emails from or to members of the State Department had to be preserved as official documents under the law and all would also be recoverable under Freedom of Information Act requests since the State Department sender or receiver had the state.gov email address.

She and her advisers might not have realized the significance of using two BlackBerrys to differentiate official from personal messages. They all should have known that when it came to official messages appropriately marked with some level of classification, it didn't matter what the email address was or whom it was to or from; it had to be communicated through a secure communications channel.

It didn't matter because if the email was designated as classified as the classification manual required—in a conspicuous header that could not be missed, with the specific level of classification stated—then it had to be sent through special secure channels from a special secure device in a Sensitive Compartmented Information Facility, a special room that was impervious to interception or hacking. That was a given.

So in a discussion about using a private email address from her BlackBerry and housing those messages on a private server, the reaction by Hillary Clinton and her advisers just might have been: no reaction. It just didn't seem at the time to be a big deal.

One BlackBerry was fine. Better. More credible. More convenient. That must have been everyone's good-faith conclusion.

So, hypothetically, shortly after she was sworn in as secretary, just suppose high in the air en route to someplace far away, let's say fifty thousand feet over Afghanistan on her way to Japan, in the middle of the night for her but perhaps while her husband and family and friends back home were just waking up, she received an urgent email message on her BlackBerry asking her a question that she believed could best be answered by someone else at State on the 24/7 desk for that particular region of the world about which the question was asked.

What did she do? Perhaps she just hit Send and forwarded it to the desk officer. She must not have thought anything about it being risky or illegal—because it was neither. There was no classified designation on the email, for it had been sent through unsecure channels by a State Department official who knew the difference between classified and unclassified, and she knew it would be preserved in two places—on her own private server in her home *and* on the state.gov server.

Still, Clinton and some of her senior aides must have wondered whether there was any precedent for using a private email system on another server outside the State Department address and server. After all, emails had become common and BlackBerrys were ubiquitous, and commercial email systems, such as AOL and CompuServe, were widely used back then. So they might have wondered whether other secretaries of state had made the same choice to use a single personal device outside the official communication system for emails not marked classified—for the same two reasons: convenience and privacy.

Several months later, they learned the answer. Yes, there was a precedent for using an outside private server, not the State Department server: former secretary of state General Colin Powell. At a dinner party several months after she became secretary, Clinton heard General Powell describe his own system when he was secretary from 2001 to 2004, similar to what she had decided to do several months before. He decided on using a desktop personal computer to send both personal and official business emails through a system outside the State Department server. He used AOL's email system and its private server. At the turn of the twenty-first century, the BlackBerry was still in rudimentary form.

Powell reminded Clinton that his reasons would be true for her too—to preserve privacy. Being Hillary Clinton, there was a real possibility that her personal emails would end up all over the Internet. He figured the emails he sent to State Department officials on the state.gov server would be preserved for posterity, as the law required, and those regarding State Department matters could be retrieved from AOL's server.

Of course, Powell said, when the emails were labeled classified, he used classified, secure channels. And that is what Hillary Clinton did as well. In any event, General Powell's comments at the dinner party confirmed for Clinton that it was okay to continue to use a single device to send her official and personal emails and to store them on a private server. Like Secretary Powell, she saw no serious security risks doing so for emails that were not marked as classified. So Clinton used her BlackBerry, never suspecting what was to happen as a result.

# CHAPTER TWO

# The *Times* Gets the Story Half-Wrong

Late in the evening of Monday, March 2, 2015, I got a call from someone in the Clinton campaign giving me a heads-up about the leading story just posted on the *New York Times* website, to be on the front page of the next morning's edition. It was about Hillary Clinton using a private email address.

The front page of the *Times* was (and is) by definition a big deal. All the news organizations, morning TV shows, and 24/7 cable news programs would be running the story as a lead or major topic for at least the next day or so.

I was told to be ready to be on TV news shows the next day, so I started to do some quick homework. When I found the story, however, I was not too concerned. The headline read, "Hillary Clinton Used Personal Email Account at State Dept., Possibly Breaking Rules."

Here is what the well-respected *Newsweek* columnist and former *Times* reporter Kurt Eichenwald subsequently wrote about this *Times* story:

> [The] highly touted article about Hillary Clinton's use of a personal email account . . . was wrong in its major points. The *Times*'s public editor defended that piece, linking to a lengthy series of regulations

that, in fact, proved the allegations contained in the article were false. While there has since been a lot of partisan hullaballoo about "email bogus-gate"—something to be expected when the story involves a political party's presidential front-runner—the reality remained that, when it came to this story, there was no there there.

When I first read the story, I came to the same conclusion. There were only three questions that interested me, substantively and politically: Was Clinton's use of private emails legal? Did she have any significant precedent of one or more prior secretaries of state who made a similar judgment that it was okay to do so? And was there any evidence of hacking or interception of her official emails by foreign adversaries such that national security had, in fact, been harmed?

The headline said only that rules had been "possibly" violated by Clinton's private email system outside the State Department. That certainly was an odd word to use in a headline, much less a front-page story. It seemed irresponsible to me, journalistically speaking. Why would the paper run a story about something "possibly" being illegal with such serious personal and political ramifications? Why not wait to see if it was, or was not, illegal?

Then came the first paragraph:

March 2, 2015, WASHINGTON—Hillary Rodham Clinton exclusively used a personal email account to conduct government business as secretary of state, State Department officials said, and may have violated federal requirements that officials' correspondence be retained as part of the agency's record.

I noticed the word "may." It weakened a declarative statement. Eichenwald seemed to agree in a *Newsweek* column he posted the following week, on March 10, titled "Why Hillary Clinton's 'Emailgate' Is a Fake Scandal." Here is what he wrote: "There is a term in journalism for the word *may*. It's called a weasel word, which helps readers gloss over what the story is really saying: That the *Times* doesn't know if the regulations were violated, but it sure sounds good to suggest that they could have been."

Then I looked at the last phrase in the paragraph about what "requirements" were "possibly" violated. Later on in the story, those requirements were further defined: "Regulations from the National Archives and Records Administration at the time required that any emails sent or received from personal accounts be preserved as part of the agency's records."

Then I was surprised to see a flat-out statement from the *Times* of a violation of these regulations by Clinton and her aides: "But Mrs. Clinton and her aides failed to do so."

What exactly had Mrs. Clinton and her aides failed to do in violation of that regulation? If they "retained" or "preserved" the records, was there a specific requirement that the records had to become part of the agency's records immediately? In other words, was there a specific time period in the Federal Records Act or in the regulations the *Times* referred to?

When I served as special White House counsel, from 1996 to 1998, we were briefed on the Federal Records Act (FRA), which required the preservation of all our official-business-related written notes and emails (in those days, there was an email system only within the White House complex, not to external individuals, so they were automatically preserved). I also had an early model of a PalmPilot—which was then called a personal digital assistant. I used it to keep telephone numbers, make appointments, and write reminder notes and telephone calls I needed to return each day.

I recalled asking an associate White House counsel who briefed us on the FRA whether I needed to immediately turn over whatever notes or records I was keeping on my PalmPilot. He said no, as long as they were preserved on the PalmPilot, I could turn them over in electronic or printed form after I left the White House. There was no time period specified in the Federal Records Act for doing so—just that they had to be "preserved."

In the third paragraph of the article, I learned that in December 2014, Clinton had turned over "55,000 pages of emails" as a result of a "new State Department effort to comply with record-keeping practices." The word "new" caught my attention. I vaguely recalled reading that the FRA had recently been amended. So I googled it and discovered that in November 2014, almost two years after Clinton had left office, the act was amended and enacted into law. The new rules set, for the first time, a specific time period after an executive official leaves office—sixty days—to turn over all official records. Prior to that, when Clinton was secretary of state, there was no official deadline.

Strange. The *Times* had omitted the rather important fact that a time period had been imposed two years *after* Secretary Clinton had left office. This apparently made the difference between legal and illegal conduct at the time she was secretary, since she had waited more than sixty days after she left office to turn them over to State.

Why hadn't the *Times* disclosed this change in the law in the article? I still figured there would have to be some legal expert to back up the paper's assertion that "Clinton and her aides" had "failed" to comply with the "requirements."

Aha. There it was: a quote from a Washington, DC, attorney, Jason R. Baron, described as having previously served as the director of litigation at the National Archives and Records Administration, which supervised and implemented the Federal Records Act to be sure federal official records were preserved for posterity and which had promulgated regulations on this issue in 2009.

"It is very difficult to conceive of a scenario—short of nuclear winter—where an agency would be justified in allowing its cabinet-level head officer to solely use a private email communications channel for the conduct of government business. . . . [Hillary Clinton's] exclusive use of her private email, for all of her work, appears unusual," Baron said.

What? That's a dramatic quote, I thought, and it caught my attention. But Baron had said "unusual," not "illegal." Similarly, another quote from him farther down in the story: "I can recall no instance in my time at the National Archives [2000–2013] when a high-ranking official at an executive branch agency solely used a personal email account for the transaction of government business."

So all the *Times* could come up with was that what Clinton had done, according to its own quoted legal expert, was "unusual"—but nothing more, no conclusion of illegality.

I was growing increasingly suspicious that the *Times* couldn't find anyone to confirm their view that Clinton had violated a law. The next day, in a post dated March 3, 3:40 P.M., I saw a headline on the *Wall Street Journal* website. It answered my question—and filled in the blanks that the *Times* had omitted. The headline: "Hillary Clinton's Personal Email Came Before Recent Rule Changes, Amendments to Federal Records Act Passed Last Year."

In the third paragraph, *Journal* reporter Brent Kendall noted that the 2014 overhaul postdated Clinton's tenure at the State Department, and he quoted from the General Services Administration rules on records management: "The law placed explicit limits on agency officials using private email accounts for official business. The new law said agency officials can't create or send a government record on a private account unless they also copy or forward the email to their official government email address."

I vividly recalled my days at the Clinton White House working with the press corps and the rivalry between the *New York Times* and the *Wall Street Journal*. Both papers liked nothing better than to one-up each other if they discovered something off in a story the other had gotten first by then writing a "gotcha" correction story. This is what it seemed the *Journal*'s Brent Kendall had done.


Coincidentally, I got my definitive answer in person from—of all people—the very expert on whom the *Times* had relied for a supportive quote. I met Jason R. Baron, the Archives Administration legal expert quoted in the *Times* story, in the greenroom at CNN on Saturday morning, March 7. He came over to introduce himself. He was scheduled to go on the influential Michael Smerconish show to discuss the emails.

"You are the attorney quoted in the *Times* story on Clinton's emails?" I asked.

"Yes, I am," he said.

"I read your quotes. I saw that you considered Clinton's use of private address emails unusual, but what is your opinion on whether they were legal or illegal?"

"Oh, no question about that. As of the time she was secretary of state, her emails using a private address were legal."

I was stunned.

"Well, why didn't you give the *Times* that quote to use in the story? That could have changed the headline that what she did was 'possibly' or 'may be' a violation of rules or requirements. You could have said that while it was 'unusual,' it wasn't in violation of the regulations or the then existing version of the Federal Records Act. Am I right?"

"I don't think the reporter ever asked me that specific question."

I asked him whether, when he wrote the 2009 regulations on the subject of records retention, there was any time specified for turning over preserved records after leaving office. And whether the law's 2014 amendment added a specific time period.

"Yes, that's right. Before then there was no time period specified in the 2009 rules to turn over the official records. After the 2014 amendments, the period was specified as sixty days."

I was amazed.

"Do you think you could clarify this and state what you just told me to Smerconish, who I am pretty sure is going to ask you about the legal issues involving Mrs. Clinton?"

"Sure," he replied, "if I am asked."

Here is what happened when Smerconish, a former practicing attorney, interviewed Baron a little while later:

SMERCONISH: What I think I'm hearing you say is that this is very unusual, but doesn't represent a violation of law. And if I misunderstood, by all means correct me.

BARON: The fact is that the 2009 regulations did not set an express deadline [to turn over emails written outside of the State Department to the department]. That deadline of twenty [he meant sixty] days to forward e-mails from a private account to an official recordkeeping system was only made part of the Federal Records Act, the statute, in 2014 after Secretary Clinton left office."

I thought that should settle the ambiguity in the *Times* story. I was confident that once Baron's conclusion on CNN that Clinton's emails were legal got picked up by other cable shows and the Internet, it would be a big story correcting the misimpression left by the *Times* story.

But that never happened. It was lost in the weekend noise and absence of media interest. Certainly, CNN didn't blast out a headline, "*Times* Key Source in CNN Interview Contradicts *Times* Story on 'Possible' Legal Violation by Hillary Clinton on Emails." Indeed, CNN never reported on anything other than the story raising questions about the legality of Clinton's private email system—along with every other mainstream media paper and TV outlet. Of course, partisan congressional Republicans immediately called for an "investigation" of Clinton. I remembered the early stages of Whitewater. As Yogi Berra is said to have said, it was déjà vu all over again.

The day after the Smerconish interview, on Sunday, March 8, the *Times*' public editor, Margaret Sullivan, weighed in. Surprisingly, since her role as a public "ombudsman" was usually to write critiques of *Times* articles that contained factual flaws, in this column she mostly defended the article from critics, whom she broadly disparaged as Clinton partisans. Indeed, to back up the reporting that Clinton's use of private emails had "possibly" violated federal "requirements," she cited the specific regulation—"section 1236.22b"—and even the specific page, "p. 51050." Impressive, I thought.

But then the next day, *Newsweek*'s Kurt Eichenwald referred to Sullivan's column and the citation and page number and then quoted from that section of the Federal Register: "'Agencies that allow employees to send and receive official electronic mail messages using a system not operated by the agency must ensure that federal records sent or received on such systems are preserved in the appropriate agency recordkeeping system.'"

And then he added: "Catch the problem? The regulation itself [cited by Sullivan], through its opening words, 'specifically designates that employees of certain agencies are allowed to use non-federal email systems.' And one of those agencies just happened to be . . . drumroll please . . . the State Department. In other words, not only was the use of a personal email account not a violation of the rules, it was specifically allowed by the rules."

So I had my answer: Clinton's private email system had been legal.

However, the emails story quickly morphed into public criticisms about Clinton's "poor judgment" in using a private system. And that led me, and many others with any logic and nonpartisan intellectual honesty, to wonder why the *New York Times* and everyone else ignored or downplayed the fact that Colin Powell had also used a private email system outside the State Department system during his tenure as secretary of state from 2001 to 2004. So on the "judgment" issue, the precedent of Secretary Powell should have been given far more attention.

On March 4, the Associated Press, in a story by Jack Gillum, broke the news that Clinton's private emails had gone through a private server maintained at her home in Chappaqua and originally set up by Bill Clinton under the supervision of his Secret Service team.

The *Times*, to its credit, did mention the Powell precedent in the March 2 story. But it downplayed its significance both in placement as well as in brevity and substance. It was impossible to miss the message that the paper did not consider the Powell precedent to be significant. Its reference to Powell did not occur until the twenty-second of twenty-eight paragraphs in the story and was limited to a single sentence: "Before the current regulations went into effect," Powell had "used personal email to communicate with American officials and ambassadors and foreign leaders." That's it. No mention that Powell had used AOL's private server to house his personal and official emails. And even that one sentence omitted the fact that the law had changed in 2014, two years after Clinton left office. We can see embedded in this first *Times* email story the errors, distortions, and half-truths pertaining to Clinton's use of emails that were then multiplied in the coverage by other mainstream media, especially the often distorted and hyped treatment on the mainstream cable news stations.

By now, everyone knows that the emails issue came to dominate the Hillary Clinton 2016 campaign as coverage of that issue eclipsed attention to her policy proposals to solve America's problems. There is also no doubt that the emails story was the single most important reason why Clinton's negative personal ratings by voters increased and positive ones decreased and why as those ratings became more negative, her poll results suffered. One question that correlated well with voter support, certainly in the days before Donald Trump became the Republican nominee, was asking all voters whether they have a "favorable" or "unfavorable" impression of Clinton. Reviewing all the data before and after the March 2, 2015, first *Times* story on emails, it is clear that the story was the turning point.

For example, prior to the *Times* story, nine out of ten favorable-versus-unfavorable polls listed on RealClearPolitics.com from January 1 to March 1 showed net positive impressions. But after the story, the results changed dramatically. Among the twenty-four polls listed between March 2 and June 1, half were net negative impressions of Clinton. And after June 1, Clinton remained net negative on voter impressions in all the RCP polls over the next eighteen months, until Election Day 2016.

On September 8, 2016, just two months before Election Day, Rep. Elijah Cummings (D-MD), ranking member of the House Committee on Oversight and Government Reform, released 2009 emails between Secretary Powell and Secretary Clinton. We learned that Powell had hooked up a personal computer to AOL and used AOL to send and receive his personal and official business emails. We learned from his own emails to Clinton that his purpose was to avoid the State Department system for privacy reasons.

"I didn't have a Blackberry," Secretary Powell said in an email to Clinton in response to her inquiry about whether she could use her BlackBerry for personal and official business communications. "What I did was have a personal computer that was hooked up to a private phone line (sounds ancient). So I could communicate with a wide range of friends directly without it going through the State Department servers. I even used it to do business with some foreign and some of the senior folks in the Department on their personal email accounts. I did the same thing on the road in hotels."

Powell seemed to understand, as the AP had reported, that using a BlackBerry would not prevent access to emails under the Freedom of Information Act (FOIA). "However," he wrote, "there is a real danger. If it is public that you have a BlackBerry and it it [*sic*] government and you are using it, government or not, to do business, it may become an official record and subject to the law."

Also, significantly, it was reported that Powell's emails had contained classified information, and so too had emails of senior aides to former secretary of state Condoleezza Rice.

So it took more than sixteen months after the *Times*' March 2, 2015, Clinton email story for all the details about Powell's use of the AOL private server to be reported. The *Times* also omitted two relevant facts that had already been published. First, on March 13, 2013, it was reported that a hacker who called himself "Guccifer" (a Romanian named Marcel-Lehel Lazar) had successfully hacked into the AOL account of Sidney Blumenthal, a friend of the Clintons who had worked in the White House as a senior adviser to President Clinton in the late 1990s. The Russian-government-controlled TV news organization, RT, first published Blumenthal's emails to Hillary Clinton at her private account address and posted all of them on March 20, 2013. Thus we also could have learned that Hillary Clinton's use of a private email address had been known for two years.

Second, a week later, on March 20, it was reported that Guccifer had hacked Secretary Colin Powell's AOL account. At the very least, if the references to the Powell precedent, his emails to Clinton, and the fact that his AOL server had been hacked had been included high up in the first March 2 *Times* story, the negative political impact on Clinton as the email story unfolded would have been much less.

In fact, the argument that Secretary Powell didn't have a private server that might have been hacked, as Secretary Clinton did, could have and should have been, "Yes, he did—but it was owned and controlled by AOL, and, unlike Clinton's private server, it was, in fact, hacked."

Such a response would have been a persuasive defense against accusations that Secretary Clinton had used "poor judgment." In fact, if the highly respected Colin Powell had used the same judgment, but on a private server that was hacked, then Hillary Clinton should not be criticized for poor judgment when there was no evidence that her private server had ever been hacked.

But the obvious point, rarely mentioned by the media, was that Clinton's private server seemed more secure than the State Department server that Republicans and media critics insisted she should have used. The AP reminded readers in its story that the State Department server had been a victim many times of Russian and Chinese hackers.

It is unclear why the *Times* missed the issue of the private server. Perhaps they didn't consider it significant. They also later missed the fact that more than 90 percent of the emails Clinton sent and received contained the state.gov address—they were between her and other State Department officials. Thus, these were automatically captured on the State Department server.

Another relevant fact was not definitively supplied until July 5, 2016, when FBI director James Comey stated that after an extensive FBI investigation, including forensic technical examinations of the hard drive of the server and all other indications that would show a successful hack or intrusion, there was "no evidence" that any successful hack had occurred—in contrast to the State Department's server. But that news came much later, and in most respects too late for Hillary Clinton.


After the *Times* story broke (and then was corrected by the *Wall Street Journal* and on CNN's Smerconish show), I underestimated the tendency of partisan Republicans who didn't particularly care about the facts and the presumption of innocence when it came to Hillary Clinton to inflate the significance of something the *Times* described as only "possibly" a rules violation. The no-fact-all-speculation negative coverage of her supposed wrongdoing regarding her use of a private email system continued for weeks, then *months*. As usual, the talking heads recycled the trite word "narrative"—that these private emails were consistent with her "penchant for secrecy"—with the same hype and repetition of the word "scandal" as seen during the Whitewater "scandal." The "coverage" was filled with sound and fury, signifying nothing.

It amazed me how few of the TV reporters even *remembered* Whitewater, much less knew that it was a classic example of a nonscandal that began that way and ended that way, notwithstanding the media hype, partisan attacks on both Clintons, and a criminal investigation lasting seven years, conducted by an independent counsel with an unlimited budget. Would they never learn the lesson of the dangers of getting ahead of the facts? Or didn't it matter, so long as column inches mounted in news stories and clicks and ratings stayed high to measure readers and viewers?

The hypercoverage was not dampened at all even after Clinton's tweet on the evening of March 4, 2015: "I want the public to see my email[s]. I asked State to release them. They said they will review them for release as soon as possible."

On the following Tuesday, March 10, Clinton made a brief statement to the assembled media after a meeting at the United Nations. There were the usual revved-up cameras, lights, working reporters crowding to get to the front and shouting questions about the emails. Clinton restated what she thought was the most important point— her commitment to transparency: She was the only secretary of state who had turned over all her official business emails to State (fifty-five thousand pages, which turned out to be about thirty thousand separate

State Department–related business emails) and that, what she and her campaign thought was significant, in her tweet the previous week she had asked all to be released to the public as soon as possible. Then she had to move on to her next event, given her tight schedule.

With the wisdom of hindsight, this might have been the tell-all moment, like the pink press conference open-to-all event, when she responded to what she thought were all questions about Whitewater, as her advisers had promised her, that would finally put the nonscandal "scandal" behind her.

She might have taken more time to respond and explain everything she could on the emails—to get "all the facts out" then and there, such as a full explanation of why she chose a private server; that she had relied on advice from and the precedent of the respected former secretary Colin Powell, who also used a private server outside the State Department; that the vast majority of the thirty thousand emails had been sent to and received by State Department officials with state .gov addresses, thus contradicting the notion that she was attempting to avoid FOIA or, for that matter, that her private email address was intended to be kept secret; and she might well have explained that since these thirty thousand emails were sent to her by senior department officials and diplomats through unsecure channels, without any classification markings, she had had no reason to view them as containing classified information any more than did all the officials and diplomats who had sent them to her through unsecure channels.

Finally, most important by far, this could have been the occasion to make the crucial distinction, which was soon missed and confused and blurred by the media, between emails properly marked, as the classification manual required, by a header with conspicuous lettering stating the level of classification status of the email versus emails that had no such header/labels at all.

This distinction was crucial because it was the classified markings that made the difference between legal and illegal—indeed, between not criminal and criminal. It is a simple fact, confirmed by FBI director Comey in his press conference of July 5, 2016, that in the absence of appropriate classified markings that were ignored by Clinton, there could not be a finding of criminal intent and, thus, no reasonable prosecutor would bring a case against her.

But to repeat: Only with the wisdom of hindsight can we see that the occasion of the UN press conference, one week after the March 2 *Times* story on "possible" rules violations, or shortly thereafter, was important. The truth is that at the time, neither I nor any other Clinton supporter I knew could take this emails story or controversy too seriously. Legal practices, with Colin Powell as precedent? Seriously? I certainly couldn't imagine this issue might last more than a few weeks. How wrong I was.

Yet for the next four months into the summer of 2015, it looked as if the emails story had gone away, fed only by the same old Hillary-hating Republican congressional partisans and far-right fringe. But then came the evening of July 23, with a new story on the front page of the *New York Times*. And everything changed.

CHAPTER THREE

# The *Times* Gets It Wrong Again

At 10:31 P.M. on Thursday, July 23, 2015, the *Times* posted a lead story on its website with the headline "Inquiry Sought in Hillary Clinton's Use of Email." The story had been written by reporters Matt Apuzzo and Michael Schmidt.

The first paragraph stated that "two inspectors general* [one from the Intelligence Community,† called the ICIG, and the other from the State Department] have asked the Justice Department to open an investigation into whether sensitive government information was mishandled in connection with the personal email account Hillary Rodham Clinton used as secretary of state."

The story was based on a July 23, 2015, memorandum that the *Times* was told by a leaker came from the two IGs recommending a "criminal referral" concerning Hillary Clinton's mishandling of her private emails. The memo was actually sent just by the Intelligence

---

* Inspectors general (IGs) are appointed by the president. They have independent authority to monitor and investigate conduct by members of any department of the executive branch. If they find wrongdoing, they can recommend disciplinary action within the department or civil or criminal investigation by the Justice Department.

† The Intelligence Community comprises sixteen intelligence agencies throughout the U.S. government, including the Central Intelligence Agency, the National Security Agency, and the Defense Intelligence Agency.

Community inspector general, I. Charles McCullough III—not also sent by the State Department inspector general, Steve A. Linick, as the *Times* wrongly reported. McCullough wrote the memo but personally signed it and sent copies to the two chairs of the House and Senate Intelligence Committees and the director of national intelligence (DNI). The full July 23, 2015, memo appears on pages 33–34.

There were actually two documents created by McCullough that had significant ramifications for Hillary Clinton and her presidential campaign. The first, not publicly available or even known to exist until two months after the 2016 presidential election, was sent to the FBI on July 6, 2015. The second was the July 23, 2015, McCullough memo to Congress and the DNI. According to a source close to McCullough,* this July 23 memo was virtually identical to the July 6 "referral" McCullough had secretly made two weeks before to the FBI.

It was this July 23 McCullough memo sent to Congress that was leaked to the *New York Times* reporters—but not the actual document itself, as the reporters subsequently admitted; just a characterization of it by someone, presumably a congressional staffer or member shortly after the document was delivered to the two intelligence committees. Mischaracterization, as we shall see, is the more accurate word.

At about seven that evening, Apuzzo had called the Justice Department to see whether it would confirm that it had received such a "criminal referral." Sometime in the next hour or so, Apuzzo received

---

* For the remainder of this and the next chapter, all references to what McCullough thought or did are a result of the author's interview with this knowledgeable source, who asked to remain anonymous because of the sensitivity of McCullough's role as Intelligence Community inspector general. He agreed to try to correct the record. McCullough's source insisted that McCullough was acting more as a "conduit" for concerns and judgments relayed to him by Intelligence Community experts, and not always expressing his own personal opinions. Yet he received the brunt of the criticisms from the Clinton campaign and supporters and Democratic members of Congress, and he could not respond to publically defend himself.

UNCLASSIFIED

INSPECTOR GENERAL OF THE INTELLIGENCE COMMUNITY
WASHINGTON, DC 20511

MEMORANDUM FOR:    SEE DISTRIBUTION

SUBJECT:    Summary of IC IG support to State Department IG

REFERENCE:    19 June 2015 Memorandum – Same Subject
                  25 June 2015 Memorandum – Same Subject

On 12 March 2015 the Inspector General (IG) of the State Department (State) received a letter from Chairmen Burr, Corker, and Johnson asking for, among other requests, a review of State employees' usage of personal email for official purposes. The letter also requested State IG coordinate with my office to determine whether classified information was transmitted or received by State employees over personal systems. In furtherance of this task, my office reviewed the procedures being used by State FOIA staff as they process approximately 30,000 emails provided by former Secretary Clinton.

**IG Recommendations.** My office discovered that an inadvertent release of classified national security information had already occurred in the State FOIA process as a result of insufficient coordination with Intelligence Community (IC) elements (State personnel continue to deny the classified character of the released information despite a definitive determination from the IC Interagency FOIA process). Consequently, State IG and I made the following four recommendations to State for improving its FOIA review process to better identify IC equities and to prevent further inadvertent releases of classified information.

1. We recommended that State involve IC FOIA officials in their FOIA review process to more readily identify IC-related classified information. They have accepted and are implementing this recommendation.

2. We recommended that the State FOIA review process be conducted on a TOP SECRET computer network. This recommendation is unresolved because, according to State, resource constraints preclude conducting the entire FOIA review on a TOP SECRET system.

3. We recommended that State FOIA officials implement a dispute resolution process in regard to differences of opinion about classification levels and

UNCLASSIFIED

UNCLASSIFIED

SUBJECT:    Update to IC IG support to State Department IG

exemptions. State has not yet provided sufficient information for us to close this recommendation.

4. We recommended that State closely coordinate with the Department of Justice throughout the FOIA process. We received assurances this coordination was occurring and have closed this recommendation.

**Additional Classified Information.** Since the referenced 25 June 2015 notification, we were informed by State FOIA officials that there are potentially hundreds of classified emails within the approximately 30,000 provided by former Secretary Clinton. We note that none of the emails we reviewed had classification or dissemination markings, but some included IC-derived classified information and should have been handled as classified, appropriately marked, and transmitted via a secure network. Further, my office's limited sampling of 40 of the emails revealed four contained classified IC information which should have been marked and handled at the SECRET level.

As I advised in my 25 June 2015 notification, the 30,000 emails in question are purported to have been copied to a thumb drive in the possession of former Secretary Clinton's personal counsel, Williams and Connelly attorney David Kendall. As my office's limited sampling identified four emails containing classified IC information, I referred this matter to counterintelligence officials at State and within the IC, including the National Counterintelligence and Security Center and the Federal Bureau of Investigation.

**Request for Copy of 30,000 Emails.** Finally, State IG and I requested a copy of the 30,000 emails in State possession so that we could perform sampling and render an independent determination of the sufficiency of the internal controls being implemented by State FOIA to protect classified national security information. State agreed to provide State IG with limited access to these 30,000 emails. However, State rejected my office's request on jurisdictional grounds.

My office will remain in contact with State IG and will be available to provide further support and assistance as State IG deems necessary. Please do not hesitate to contact me with any questions or concerns, at 571-204-8149.

I. Charles McCullough, III
Inspector General of the Intelligence Community

7/23/2015
Date

DISTRIBUTION:    The Honorable Richard Burr
The Honorable Dianne Feinstein
The Honorable Devin Nunes
The Honorable Adam Schiff
The Honorable James Clapper, Director of National Intelligence

UNCLASSIFIED

2

a call back from the Justice Department official he had talked to and received a confirmation. The *Times* called others at Justice and obtained other confirmations. Based on those confirmations, the *Times* posted the story on its website that night and on its front page the next morning, July 24.

News that Hillary Clinton was under criminal investigation because of her emails was a big deal. The story spread rapidly across the Internet that night. It dominated coverage on front pages across the nation and lead stories on news websites. It went viral on Twitter and other social media. It led all the morning TV shows, with the inevitable BREAKING NEWS crawling across the screens of cable news shows. However, by midday on Friday, Justice shocked everyone. It withdrew its prior "confirmations" to the *Times* and other news organizations it had made only a few hours earlier. It stated that there had not been a "criminal referral" as they had previously stated, but rather a "security referral"—without explaining what that latter term meant.

Then something even more unusual happened. The two inspector generals, McCullough and Linick, who rarely spoke to the media at all, issued a joint public statement echoing the Justice Department's contradiction of the *Times* story that they had made a "criminal referral" about Hillary Clinton and her private email system. They made the same distinction—there was no "criminal referral," but rather a "security referral."

The *Washington Post* immediately posted a story explaining what a "security referral" was—a routine dispute between agencies as to what Clinton emails should or should not be released under the Freedom of Information Act (FOIA). The *Post* reported: "McCullough [the ICIG] said he also recommended that freedom-of-information officials at the State Department implement 'a dispute resolution process [involving the Intel Community, State, and the FBI] in regard to differences of opinion about classification levels and exemptions.'"

So if this was what the *Times* story was really about, then what was all the fuss about? How did it merit a rushed posting by the *Times* late on Thursday night and then front-page treatment in the July 24 morning paper? And how did the *Times* reporters, two of the most outstanding reporters in Washington, get the core fact wrong that there was no criminal referral made by McCullough, much less made by "two IGs"? By midday, after repudiation of the story by both Justice and the IGs, obviously the *Times* had to withdraw the story that Clinton was personally under criminal investigation. Condemnations of both the *Times* and the Justice Department for getting something so important so wrong, unfairly damaging Clinton's presidential candidacy, poured in from all over the media and from the Clinton campaign. The *Times* was faulted by its own public editor for the "rush to publish," and many others criticized Justice for the "rush to confirm." The criticism was even worse when the *Times'* public editor several days later acknowledged that the paper's reporters had not seen the July 23 memo that was the basis for their entire story, even though the reporters said that they relied on confirmations of what they had been told from multiple sources at the Justice Department.

Virtually everyone following the presidential campaign had the same questions: What the heck had happened? The *Times* gets confirmations, Justice reverses itself, and two inspectors general issue a public statement rebutting a newspaper story?

These questions had answers, albeit troubling and only completely understandable two months after the election, when the FBI first posted on its "public vault" of website documents that had previously remained undisclosed. (They will be explained in the next chapter.)

Let's start with how the *Times* reported this story and how it got it so wrong. We begin during the afternoon and evening of July 23, inside the sausage factory process among a national newspaper trying to confirm a leak, a presidential campaign not knowing the substance of the leak, and the Justice Department hastily "confirming" the story.

That afternoon, Brian Fallon, the national press secretary for the Clinton campaign, received a call from *Times* reporter Schmidt. Before joining the Clinton campaign, Fallon had served as public affairs director at the Department of Justice under Attorney General Eric Holder. Schmidt was a widely respected young reporter who had been covering Congress, including the Benghazi special committee work and hearings. Schmidt asked Fallon if he had heard about a memo or some written communication from "two IGs" from the State Department and the Intel Community raising the possibility of classified material traversing Secretary Clinton's email system.

Fallon, a pro when it came to reading and interpreting journalists, had the impression that Schmidt was fishing. He didn't seem to have any hard information and was looking to "feed" from Fallon's reaction the story he didn't yet have. But Fallon had no idea what Schmidt was talking about and told him so. Schmidt said he would call Fallon back before writing a story. Fallon at that point did nothing further, as he didn't take Schmidt's call seriously.

Unbeknownst to Fallon, a couple of hours later, at about 6:30 or 7 P.M., Apuzzo, the other *Times* reporter working on the same story, whose primary beat was the Justice Department, called a junior Justice official who dealt with the media. Apuzzo asked for confirmation that the department had received a written criminal referral from two IGs of Intel and State seeking a "criminal investigation" of Hillary Clinton over her handling of her emails.

This official was not a lawyer. (To maintain the promised anonymity of the former Justice Department officials who were sources for this account, I will use the pronoun "he" for all, even though the gender could be male or female.) The junior official called a senior department official, an attorney who worked near the level of the attorney general. He asked whether Clinton was under criminal investigation. The senior official paused, then said yes, he could confirm.

"Are you sure?" the junior official asked. He knew that confirming to Apuzzo would trigger a major *Times* story. Announcing that Hillary Clinton was under criminal investigation could be a game changer affecting the election. We had better be right in confirming, he thought. We can always give no comment tonight and wait to see whether we can get more information tomorrow morning, he said to the senior official.

The senior official said he would check with others and call back, which he did shortly thereafter. He told the junior official that he had spoken to another department official. "He said I could confirm the criminal referral, saying, 'It is what it is.'" The senior official also added, vaguely, that he had gotten the same confirmation from an FBI official.

So the junior official, still with serious doubts, called Apuzzo back at about 8 P.M. on July 23 and said he had gotten confirmation of a criminal referral about Clinton's emails.

At 8:36, Schmidt called Fallon back. Unlike his earlier call in the afternoon, Schmidt now sounded far more definite and ready to go with a story. He told Fallon that the *Times* had received a "separate tip" that two IGs had sent a criminal referral to Justice about Hillary Clinton being under investigation over her emails. (Fallon had a hunch the leak came from someone on Capitol Hill. He guessed it was someone from the House Benghazi Committee, since that was the committee Schmidt had covered previously.)

Fallon's adrenaline spiked along with his heartbeat. If true, this was very serious; it could represent a grave threat to the Clinton campaign, which, in the summer of 2015, was already in a competitive contest with Vermont senator Bernie Sanders for the nomination.

Fallon told Schmidt he hadn't heard anything about a criminal referral to Justice about Clinton. He thought it was implausible since he figured someone from the legal advisers to Clinton (or himself, as a former Justice Department official) would have heard about it, even vaguely. Fallon asked Schmidt how certain was he about the truth of this tip. Had he challenged the "tipster" to show him the document that was the basis of the tip? No answer.

Fallon still had a feeling that Schmidt didn't have it all completely nailed down and hadn't seen the document that had triggered his call. Fallon asked whether he could have more time to check this out with senior campaign officials. Schmidt said that was fine, that Fallon "had time," suggesting publication of the story was not imminent.

Despite the late hour—it was close to nine o'clock, and Fallon was now alone at Clinton's Brooklyn campaign headquarters, still not having eaten dinner—Fallon knew he needed to immediately assemble the high command of the campaign. He called communications director Jennifer Palmieri, who had gone out to dinner, and told her about the most recent call from Schmidt. She immediately returned to Clinton HQ. Palmieri and Fallon organized a conference call of senior advisers and lawyers. Fallon told everyone what Schmidt had said and asked whether anyone knew anything. The answer was no. He asked everyone to check with their sources at Justice and Capitol Hill and get back to him ASAP. He heard back not too long after: No one had heard anything.

Fallon was relieved. If Justice was initiating a criminal investigation of Hillary Clinton, Fallon, a veteran of breaking news stories, believed there would have been various leaks already occurring and maybe other news organizations chasing the same leak.

Fallon was certain of one thing: Schmidt and the *Times* would not go with a story of such importance and potential damage to Clinton's presidential candidacy without calling back to seek a comment, and perhaps share the basis of the information that had been confirmed as true.

Meanwhile, Apuzzo had apparently received confirmation of the criminal referral from other sources at Justice. Even though neither he nor Schmidt had read the July 23 memo that had been characterized by the "tipster" as a "criminal referral," both reporters were confident that they had multiple sources at the Justice Department confirming the story.

When Fallon hadn't heard back from Schmidt after 10 P.M., he was a little concerned. At 10:36, he attempted to call Schmidt on his cell phone. No answer. He left a voice mail. But Fallon was still confident that there could be no story written before he heard back from Schmidt. The *Times* and Schmidt would never do such a thing, he thought.

Eighteen minutes later, Fallon called again. Voice mail again. Fallon left another message. He was now more concerned.

Just before eleven o'clock, Fallon's cell phone rang. It was Schmidt. "I assume you are not writing and still checking out the 'tip,'" Fallon said.

Schmidt replied, "Sorry, that's not correct. The story has just been published on the *Times* website."

"What?" asked Fallon. He hung up in a fury. He and Palmieri immediately went to the *Times* website. They were horrified to see the headline and story that Hillary Clinton was under criminal investigation at the request of two IGs for possibly mishandling sensitive information on her private emails.

Fallon was angry at Schmidt and the *Times* for violating what he thought was a fundamental rule of fairness between a journalist and a source: You don't publish a story that could do damage to anyone, much less a front-running presidential candidate, without calling and giving the subject a chance to respond.

Fallon immediately called Schmidt to express his anger. He also spoke to Apuzzo. It was apparent to Fallon that neither reporter had read the memo from the IGs that seemed to be the basis for the "tip" they had received. Fallon still didn't know that Justice Department officials had already confirmed the story.

After heated discussion back and forth, with each reporter separately hearing Fallon's protests that they didn't have a hard confirmation that Hillary Clinton was under personal criminal investigation, Fallon sensed that aspect of their story might be shaky. A short time later, by then near midnight on July 23, Fallon learned that the *Times* had filed a revised version of the story, deleting the personal reference to Clinton as the subject of the criminal investigation. The revised version switched to a passive tense, omitting Clinton's name—now the "criminal referral" by the "two IGs" was about "whether a sensitive government investigation was mishandled."

But the *Times* made this subtle tense change in the story without informing the readers at the time. (Four days later, on July 27, a relatively lengthy Editors' Note acknowledged that the failure to inform the readers of the deletion of Hillary Clinton as a personal subject of the investigation was an error.) However, that change didn't help Clinton at all.

The story as first posted, with "criminal investigation" in the headline, was repeated across mainstream websites and social media overnight and on all the Friday morning network and cable news shows. The Clinton campaign's frantic efforts to inform other media outlets about the deletion of Hillary Clinton as personally the subject of the "referral" were ineffectual.

The damage was done. As the *Times* public editor put it in her lengthy July 27 critique of the article, "You can't put stories like this back in the bottle—they ripple through the entire news system."

The next morning, at the usual early morning senior staff meeting attended by top Justice Department officials, no one in the room offered any objections to the *Times* story. Other news organizations—as well as the *Times* again—called the Justice Department that morning and got the same confirmation that had been given to the *Times* the night before.

Meanwhile, according to a close source to ICIG McCullough, he was unaware of the *Times'* front-page story in the early morning of July 24, and was driving on the Washington, DC, Beltway, heading for his Virginia office, when his cell phone rang. It was State's IG, Steve Linick.

"Have you seen this morning's *Times*?" Linick reportedly asked.

"Not yet," McCullough is said to have replied. McCullough pulled over to look at his phone.

"There's a real shit storm going on," Linick is reported to have said. "Neither of us made a criminal referral about Hillary Clinton and emails—am I right?"

McCullough scanned the *Times* story. He may have said words that would require an "expletive deleted" expression. "No, of course not," McCullough said. The referral he had made early in the month to the FBI, and summarized in his July 23 memo to Congress, was about bolstering State's efforts to review Clinton's emails for possible classified information before any decisions on disclosure should be made under FOIA. That was a security referral, not a criminal referral, he said.

Both McCullough and Linick reportedly knew they had to do something fast to correct the misreporting by the *Times* and calm down the "shit storm." McCullough raced to his office of the ICIG in northern Virginia to begin drafting a corrective statement, reportedly also in touch with the Justice Department about what he and Linick were working on to correct the misreporting.

Meanwhile, Justice officials, embarrassed about their erroneous confirmation to the *Times* the night before that the two IGs had made a criminal referral, were also at work on a corrective statement. Sources report that by then they actually had read a copy of the McCullough July 23 memo to Congress. It didn't take long to read the two-page document and to see that there was no "criminal referral" mentioned. So the difficult and embarrassing decision was made at senior levels at Justice to reverse its prior confirmations. The junior official who had confirmed to Apuzzo the night before heard the news and called Apuzzo immediately to tell him. He deserved to hear first, the official explained. His reaction was not positive.

At 12:15 P.M. on Friday, the Justice Department announced its retraction of its prior confirmations of a "criminal referral" by the

ICIG. Rather, they described it, for some reason without further explanation, as a "security referral." The media reaction critical of Justice was severe not only for the department's haste to confirm but also its failure to explain its reversal.


At about the same time, the two IGs—ICIG McCullough and State's IG Linick—issued their unusual joint public statement directly contradicting the *Times* front-page story that morning, saying they had not made a "criminal referral" regarding Hillary Clinton's handling of the emails, but rather a "security referral" for "counterintelligence purposes."

A close examination of this crucial joint July 24 public statement by the two IGs sheds light on a lot of the subsequent misreporting on the Clinton email issue by mainstream media through the rest of Hillary Clinton's campaign. The key reporting errors made by the mainstream media can be seen, in retrospect, to go back to the distinction between a noncriminal "security referral" versus a criminal referral. The media consistently failed to report the crucial distinction between Clinton emails that had no appropriate classified markings and those unmarked emails that were described as "containing classified information," based on post-facto judgments by some Intel Community members that were, at the very least, subject to debate and that occurred in a tiny fraction (well below 1 percent) of the thirty thousand plus Clinton State Department emails sent to her private server. The distinction is crucial: between what was legal versus what was illegal.

Now let's examine the key sentences of the July 24 public statement by the two IGs with comments about their implications for the handling of the Clinton email issue by the media for the remainder of the campaign:

Yesterday [July 23] the Office of the Inspector General of the Intelligence Community (ICIG) sent a congressional notification to intelligence oversight committees updating them of the ICIG support to the State Department IG (attached).

The ICIG found four emails containing classified IC-derived information in a limited sample of 40 emails of the 30,000 emails provided by former Secretary Clinton. The four emails, which have not been released through the State FOIA process, did not contain classification markings and/or dissemination controls.

Note no "classification markings and/or dissemination controls" on four out of forty. These four emails were identified after an inspector in McCullough's IG office in Virginia visited the State Department for two days at the end of June and reviewed the thirty thousand plus Clinton emails. He was forced to stop after two days but was allowed to take a sample of forty emails that he believed might "possibly" include classified information. Subsequently, Intel Community experts reviewed these forty and identified four that they believed contained classified information.

As we shall see, although this sample was only forty out of thirty thousand, at the end of the year-long FBI investigation, *none* of the thirty thousand Clinton emails would be found to have appropriate classification markings. This was confirmed by the source close to ICIG McCullough. Yet the crucial distinction between documents appropriately marked and not marked was either ignored or confused by Republicans, intentionally conflated to suggest that unmarked documents could be the basis of criminal prosecution. Note also that the reference to "30,000 emails provided by former Secretary Clinton" does not distinguish between emails she received from others and simply forwarded and those she created. We now know that most of the more than three hundred senior State Department officials sent Hillary Clinton emails through unsecure channels, using the state.gov system. Therefore, these officials did not believe the emails contained any classified information. In his July 23 memo, the ICIG seemed focused only on Secretary Clinton's transfer of the emails to her private server, and not the more than three hundred diplomats who sent her these emails through the state.gov unsecure system. Why?

> These emails were not retroactively classified by the State Department; rather these emails contained [unmarked] classified information when they were generated and, according to IC classification officials, that information remains classified today. This classified information should never have been transmitted via an unclassified personal system.

While this sentence states that the "classified information should never have been transmitted via an unclassified personal system," the statement omits the word "unmarked"—which was not disputed by McCullough. Indeed, according to the knowledgeable source, McCullough was not aware of any Clinton emails that were appropriately marked as required by the Classified Manual. McCullough would not dispute that his use of the word "should" in "should never have been transmitted" is based on the subjective judgment of some Intel Community officials who made that judgment—a judgment that was vulnerable to dispute by other experts at State and elsewhere.

In fact, the judgment regarding those four emails was disputed by experts at State. Some reports had State disputing all four—i.e., none of them contained classified information at the time they were transmitted to Clinton and that is why they were not marked and not transmitted through secure channels. This dispute between the Intelligence Community, which has a record of overclassifying, and the State Department, which leans in the direction of transparency, is long-standing and not surprising. For example, the media later reported that the ICIG claimed that an email that included published reports in the *New York Times* "should have been" marked classified. A published report available online immediately should have been marked classified, according to ICIG McCullough? Seriously? Therefore, just because someone in the Intelligence Community claims a document meets the standards of classification status doesn't make it so. Far from it. This point was almost always missed by mainstream media headlining that Clinton's emails contained "classified" information.

The source close to McCullough said that McCullough recognized there could be good faith disagreements in classification judgments—that such judgments were an "art, not science."

Jeffrey Toobin, in an August 18, 2015, commentary in the *New Yorker* titled "Hillary's Problem: The Government Classifies Everything," referred to the great New York senator Daniel Patrick Moynihan and his book *Secrecy: The American Experience* to make this point about the Intel Community's tendency to overclassify: "Classified information is supposed to be defined as material that would damage national security if released," Toobin wrote. "In fact, Moynihan asserted, government bureaucracies use classification rules to protect turf, to avoid embarrassment, to embarrass rivals—in short, for a variety of motives that have little to do with national security. As the senator wrote, 'Americans are familiar with the tendency to overregulate in other areas. What is different with secrecy is that the public cannot know the extent of the content of the regulation. Thus, secrecy is the ultimate mode of regulation; the citizen does not even know that he or she is being regulated!'"

McCullough's public statement went on to say that "the ICIG made a referral detailing the potential compromise of classified information to security officials within the Executive Branch. The main purpose of the referral was to notify security officials that classified information may exist on at least one private server and thumb drive that are not in the government's possession."

The word "potential" means exactly that. So does "may." There was no finding that the "classified information" had in fact been "compromised" when it was transferred to a "private server" or to a "thumb drive." The former is a clear reference to Hillary Clinton's private server. The latter refers to a small memory device containing Clinton's thirty thousand emails, in the possession of Clinton's personal attorney, David Kendall, at the distinguished Washington law firm of Williams & Connolly. No one has ever suggested there was anything improper in Kendall, a highly respected attorney, retaining copies of all his client's emails on a thumb drive that he kept under lock and key at his law offices. Yet this seemed to trouble ICIG McCullough enough that he mentioned it both in the July 23 memo as well as in the public statement issued the following day. Why?

As to Clinton's private server, we know from Comey's press conference a year later, on July 5, 2016, that an extensive FBI technical/forensic investigation found "no evidence" of any successful hacking or compromise of Clinton's server. Yet even in the absence of such evidence, ICIG McCullough rang the alarm bell of a "compromise" requiring an interagency "counterintelligence" "security referral." Why?

Then the two IGs addressed the key question—did either make a "criminal referral" to the FBI about Clinton's email practices? The answer, unequivocally, was no.

> An important distinction is that the ICIG did not make a criminal referral [to the Justice Department]—it was a security referral made for counterintelligence purposes.

This is the most crucial sentence in the entire document—the one that contradicted and embarrassed the *New York Times*. And this was the key sentence, according to the source familiar with McCullough's thinking, that McCullough and Linick knew had to be issued immediately to quell the "shit storm."

> The ICIG is statutorily required to refer potential compromises of national security information to the appropriate IC security officials.

This appears to be a reference to the referral McCullough had made to the FBI two weeks before. As we shall see in the next chapter, this "noncriminal" referral by McCullough was referenced as a possible basis for the FBI to open a "full" criminal investigation of Clinton's handling of emails. However, the source close to McCullough stated that it was never McCullough's intent to initiate a criminal investigation of Clinton. In fact, he did not know that such a criminal investigation of Clinton had been opened until he read about it in the media months later.

Here is the only sentence in McCullough's July 23 memo to the congressional intelligence committees that contains a reference to a referral to the FBI:

> As my office's limited sampling identified four emails containing classified IC information, I referred this matter to counterintelligence officials at State and within the IC, including the National Counterintelligence and Security Center and the Federal Bureau of investigation.

Note that there is no word "criminal" in this sentence.

This is probably the sentence that the leaker of the McCullough July 23 memo to the *Times* either misunderstood or intentionally mischaracterized—i.e., wrongly inferring that since there was a reference to the FBI in the memo, that must have meant that McCullough was making a "criminal referral." Wrong. In fact, the sentence includes not only a reference to the FBI in its noncriminal counterintelligence role to review documents for possible classification status, but also to the State Department and the National Counterintelligence and Security Center as well—omitted by the *Times* in its erroneous reporting.

Meanwhile, what did the *Times* do after it realized that the two IGs had publicly contradicted its reporting by midafternoon on July 24? One would have expected the *Times* to publish a "clean-up" version that was strictly factual and balanced. Such a report would have described the full context of the ICIG's July 23 memo—specifically, the preceding six memos between McCullough and the State Department IG and the State Department, primarily about FOIA disclosure issues. Three memos from the two IGs out of the total of six mentioned "FOIA Processes" in the subject line. In short, the *Times* could have amplified the meaning of a "security referral," explaining that this was mostly about a typical FOIA dispute between the Intel Community and the State Department, in which the FBI was playing a noncriminal, "security referral" role, and that would have been the end of that.

Instead, the *Times* ran a story on the afternoon of July 24 with this headline: "Hillary Clinton Emails Said to Contain Classified Data." Note that the headline does not specify that the classified data was not labeled as such. Then came the first sentence to support the headline: "Government investigators said Friday that they had discovered classified information on the private email account that Hillary Rodham Clinton used as secretary . . ."

The article went on to discuss classified information, but it wasn't until the seventh paragraph that we learn the significant fact that Clinton's emails were "not marked classified."

The article continued: "The two investigators did not say whether Mrs. Clinton sent or received the emails [that contained classified information]. If she received them, it is not clear that she would have known that they contained government secrets, since they were not marked classified."

Finally, toward the end, the reporters seemed to imply that Clinton was guilty of *something*: "Irrespective of terminology, the referral raises the possibility of a Justice Department investigation into Mrs. Clinton's emails as she campaigns for president. . . . Mishandling classified information is a crime. Justice Department officials said no decision has been made about whether to open a criminal investigation."

There are no new facts here, just innuendo—"raises the possibility" is a classic example. This on the same day as the Justice Department and the two IGs had contradicted the *Times* report that the two IGs had made a "criminal referral."

What are we to make of the reminder that "mishandling classified information is a crime"? Well, of course it is. "Mishandling" by definition means sending clearly marked "classified" documents through unsecure channels, whether using the unsecure state.gov emails system or a private server. But since the story already stated that so far none of Clinton's emails reviewed were marked, then what was the purpose of this gratuitous statement?

And then the next sentence, that the Justice Department had said "no decision has been made" whether to open an investigation. What is the point of reporting what the Justice Department has decided not to do *yet*? It is hard to avoid the conclusion that this final July 24 *Times* story seemed to be more about vindication and argument than straight fact reporting, with the overall effect to suggest that, well, we might have been wrong about Hillary Clinton being under criminal investigation now, but . . . just wait . . . it won't be too long.

It was almost as if the *Times* was *predicting* something. Little did the paper's editors and reporters know that something already *had* happened—but nobody in the public knew about it until after the 2016 presidential election was over.

A number of media observers and even some other newspapers expressed concerns about the *Times'* coverage of the Clinton campaign emails. It wasn't just that the stories on March 2 and July 23 seemed almost overanxious to push the negative side of the envelope. It appeared the *Times* was ready to ignore positive facts and, as seen in the July 24 story, went out of their way to include negative implications about Clinton even at the expense of omitting positive facts contained later.

Josh Marshall, whose *Talking Points Memo* is one of the best and most thoughtful blogs, wrote this about the *Times* on the evening of July 24, reacting to the paper's July 23 story and the events of July 24:

> As I noted this afternoon, a lot of this has a disturbing similarity to the *Times*' Whitewater coverage—which dominated much of the Clinton presidency and turned out to be either vastly over-hyped or in numerous cases simply false. And this is the *Times*! What's supposedly the best paper in the country.
>
> Does this happen because reporters get too in the habit of accepting opposition research leads and leaks and the stories are just too good to be true? Is the hunger for the big blockbuster too great? These are genuine hypotheticals because the reporters on this story are not hacks by a longshot. But the errors in this story seem so dramatic and so easily checkable that I feel like there's something up at the *Times*. Not something nefarious, I don't think. But some unexamined institutional bias, some over-haste to push out stories based on leaks from interested parties. *Something*. Because as it stands, it's not just that the story doesn't add up. We know that. They've admitted that. How this mistake got made doesn't add up either.

There are legitimate questions raised by Josh Marshall's comment about an unconscious *Times* mind-set when it comes to Bill and Hillary Clinton over more than two decades. Was anything learned from all the time and attention and energy devoted by the *Times* and the other mainstream media to reporting on the Whitewater "scandal"?

Apparently not. As noted, the incessant, largely inaccurate, and innuendo-laced coverage of Clinton's emails drove up her personal negatives among many voters beginning with the first *Times* story in early March 2015. This occurred across all mainstream media—print, Internet, and especially cable news (where the hype and ratings-chasing,

breathless BREAKING NEWS alerts were probably worse than elsewhere).

The *Washington Post*'s editorial of September 8, 2016, eloquently
foresaw the possible consequences of this overhyped and disproportionate coverage of the Clinton emails (addressed not just to the *New
York Times* but also to all the journalists who had been covering the
emails during the campaign):

> Judging by the amount of time NBC's Matt Lauer spent pressing
> Hillary Clinton on her emails during Wednesday's national security
> presidential forum, one would think that her homebrew server was
> one of the most important issues facing the country this election.
> It is not. There are a thousand other substantive issues—from
> China's aggressive moves in the South China Sea to National Security
> Agency intelligence-gathering to military spending—that would have
> revealed more about what the candidates know and how they would
> govern. Instead, these did not even get mentioned in the first of
> 5 ½ precious prime-time hours the two candidates will share before
> Election Day, while emails took up a third of Ms. Clinton's time.
>
> Sadly, Mr. Lauer's widely panned handling of the candidate forum
> was not an aberration. Judging by polls showing that voters trust
> Donald Trump more than Ms. Clinton, as well as other evidence, it
> reflects a common shorthand for this election articulated by NFL
> quarterback Colin Kaepernick last week: "You have Donald Trump,
> who's openly racist," he said. Then, of Ms. Clinton: "I mean, we
> have a presidential candidate who's deleted emails and done things
> illegally and is a presidential candidate. That doesn't make sense
> to me, because if that was any other person, you'd be in prison."
>
> In fact, Ms. Clinton's emails have endured much more scru-
> tiny than an ordinary person's would have, and the criminal case
> against her was so thin that charging her would have been to treat

her very differently. Ironically, even as the email issue consumed so much precious airtime, several pieces of news reported Wednesday should have taken some steam out of the story. First is a memo FBI Director James B. Comey sent to his staff explaining that the decision not to recommend charging Ms. Clinton was "not a cliff-hanger" and that people "chest-beating" and second-guessing the FBI do not know what they are talking about. Anyone who claims that Ms. Clinton should be in prison accuses, without evidence, the FBI of corruption or flagrant incompetence.

Second is the emergence of an email exchange between Ms. Clinton and former secretary of state Colin Powell in which he explained that he used a private computer and bypassed State Department servers while he ran the agency, even when communicating with foreign leaders and top officials. Mr. Powell attempted last month to distance himself from Ms. Clinton's practices, which is one of the many factors that made the email story look worse. Now it seems, Mr. Powell engaged in similar behavior.

Last is a finding that 30 Benghazi-related emails that were recovered during the FBI email investigation and recently attracted big headlines had nothing significant in them. Only one, in fact, was previously undisclosed, and it contained nothing but a compliment from a diplomat. But the damage of the "30 deleted Benghazi emails" story has already been done.

Ms. Clinton is hardly blameless. She treated the public's interest in sound record-keeping cavalierly. A small amount of classified material also moved across her private server. But it was not obviously marked as such, and there is still no evidence that national security was harmed. Ms. Clinton has also admitted that using the personal server was a mistake. The story has vastly exceeded the boundaries of the facts.

Imagine how history would judge today's Americans if, looking back at this election, the record showed that voters empowered a dangerous man because of . . . a minor email scandal. There is no equivalence between Ms. Clinton's wrongs and Mr. Trump's manifest unfitness for office.

*Esquire*'s Charles Pierce wrote on September 9, 2016, an article about this editorial, headlined "*The Washington Post* Just Declared War on *The New York Times.*" Then on April 18, 2017, Pierce added these comments about the *Times*' history of critical coverage of Bill and Hillary Clinton:

> The fact is that the *Times* and the Clintons have been locked in this solipsistic dance of destruction ever since Jeff Gerth wrote the first botched story [in March 1992] about Whitewater during the 1992 presidential campaign. It has defined the newspaper and the family, one to another. Somehow, Being Tough on the Clintons has become one of the ways the *Times* has tried to prove its journalistic *bona fides* to the country and the world. . . .
>
> The dysfunction has gone on so long that hardly anyone remembers how it began—which was the aforementioned Whitewater story and everything that came after it, including some truly odious work by the late William Safire, who beat his little tin drum not only on Whitewater, but on TravelGate, FileGate, and whatever other fantasies he was fed by the Republicans in Congress and by the sieve that was Ken Starr's office.
>
> In one 1996 column, Safire memorably called HRC "a congenital liar," and in January of 1997, he assured his readers that indictments were imminent on the FileGate story. They were not, but Indictments Are Imminent became a genre of the *Times*' Clinton coverage unto the most recent campaign, as we shall see.

I am not suggesting that the *New York Times* was knowingly biased against Hillary Clinton. The *Times* remains one of the world's greatest news organizations, and its current generation of reporters live up to that standard and surely should not be blamed for the over-the-top coverage of Whitewater in the 1990s or the apparently unedited bile of Maureen Dowd on the editorial pages. But the objective facts are that the *Times* emails coverage, and all the other media's coverage of the Clinton emails, is fairly subject to challenge—and, as predicted by the *Washington Post*'s editorial board, holds some responsibility for the election of what we now know is a dangerous man to the White House. However, it is also fair to note that the *Times* editorial board endorsed Hillary Clinton's candidacies in her races for the Senate in 2000 and 2006 and her presidential campaigns of 2008 and 2016.

Of course it is still a fact—the core fact of this book—that despite all the inflated and distorted press coverage of Clinton's emails*[1]; despite various mistakes she made before and during the campaign, including, by her own admission, the decision to use a private email address stored on a private server; despite, too, the various second-guessed decisions by the Hillary Clinton campaign managers, some whose brilliant minds-by-hindsight were quick to anonymously whisper into the ears of authors and journalists to critique the campaign—yes, despite all this, according to all the respected polls, if the election had been held on October 27, 2016, Hillary Clinton would be in the White House today and Donald Trump would perhaps be tweeting that Hillary Clinton was actually not an American citizen.

Let's look closer at the key players who set the wheels in motion: the FBI, led by James Comey, who ordered its criminal investigation;

* For example, a September 2017 study by Harvard and MIT scholars titled "Partisanship, Propaganda, and Disinformation: Online Media and the 2016 U.S. Presidential Election" concluded that "the majority of mainstream media coverage was negative for both candidates, but largely followed Donald Trump's agenda: when reporting on Hillary Clinton, coverage primarily focused on the various scandals related to the Clinton Foundation and emails. When focused on Trump, major substantive issues, primarily immigration, were prominent."

the inspector general of the Intelligence Community, McCullough, who seemed unusually active in the series of events leading up to that investigation; and finally, the Justice Department, whose leaders failed to do their job of ensuring that Comey understood he was not an independent agency or power outside of our constitutional democracy but was subject to the department's supervision and policies.

# CHAPTER FOUR

# The FBI Criminal Investigation

It was Sunday night, January 8, 2017, exactly two months to the day after the election of Donald Trump. The FBI chose that time, when fewer people are online, to post three hundred pages of the records from its Hillary Clinton emails criminal investigation on its website, called its FOIA Vault.

Among these posted documents were three important ones. The first was a July 10, 2015, FBI memo opening a criminal investigation of Hillary Clinton and her email practices. This memo, which appears on pages 58–60, claimed the decision was based on "documentation" provided by the ICIG, Charles McCullough, in a July 6 referral sent to the FBI. In other words, the *New York Times* got the fact of an FBI criminal investigation *right* in their July 23 story. What they got wrong was the *source* of the decision to investigate. It wasn't the two IGs who asked for a criminal investigation, as reported by the *Times*, but the FBI.

But on April 22, 2017, in a lengthy front-page story, bylined in part by Apuzzo and Schmidt, the *Times* reporters seemed to be minimizing the errors made in the July 23 story as more about semantics and a technical error than that the facts were wrong or they had broken any rules of Journalism 101.

In fact, some facts were wrong, and they appear to have violated fundamental rules that journalists usually try to follow. They should

FD-1057 (Rev 5-8-10)     ~~SECRET~~ / ~~NOFORN~~

**OFFICIAL RECORD**

# FEDERAL BUREAU OF INVESTIGATION
### Electronic Communication

**Title:** (U//~~FOUO~~) Opening of Full Investigation on     **Date:** 07/10/2015
a Sensitive Investigative Matter (SIM)

**CC:** [                    ]

**From:** COUNTERINTELLIGENCE
         D5-CD4

  **Contact:** [                    ]

**Approved By:** [                    ]
         SC KABLE CHARLES H IV
         A/DAD David W Archey
         AD COLEMAN RANDALL C

**Drafted By:** [                    ]

**Case ID #:** [                    ] Serial 1
                              (S/~~NF~~) [                    ]
         MISHANDLING OF CLASSIFIED;
         UNKNOWN SUBJECT OR COUNTRY;
         SENSITIVE INVESTIGATIVE MATTER (SIM)

FBI INFO.
CLASSIFIED BY: NSICG J57J85T94     b6
REASON: 1.4 (C)                    b7C
DECLASSIFY ON: 12-31-2040
DATE: 10-27-2016

b6
b7C

b6
b7C

b1
b3
b7E

### DOCUMENT RESTRICTED TO CASE PARTICIPANTS
This document contains information that is restricted to case participants.

**Synopsis:** (U) (S/NF) FBIHQ, Counterespionage Section, is opening a full
investigation based on specific articulated facts provided by an 811
referral from the Inspector General of the Intelligence Community,
dated July 6, 2015 regarding the potential compromise of classified
information.

         Reason: 1.4(c)
         Derived From: Multiple (U)
         ~~Sources~~
         Declassify On: 20401231

**Full Investigation Initiated:** 07/10/2015

~~SECRET~~ / ~~NOFORN~~

~~SECRET~~//~~NOFORN~~

Title: (U//~~FOUO~~) Opening of Full Investigation on a Sensitive
Investigative Matter (SIM)
Re: [                    ] 07/10/2015

b3
b7E

**Enclosure(s):** Enclosed are the following items:
1. (U//~~FOUO~~) Referral documents received from ICIG

**Details:**

(U) (~~S//NF~~) FBIHQ, Counterespionage Section, is opening a full investi
gation based on specific articulated facts provided by an 811 referral
from the Inspector General of the Intelligence Community (ICIG), dated
July 6, 2015 regarding the potential compromise of classified
information.

(U//~~FOUO~~) The purpose of this investigation is to detect, obtain
information about, and protect against federal crimes or threats to the
national security. The initiation of this Full Investigation is based,
as per AGG-Dom II.B.3 and DIOG Section 7.5, on activity constituting a
federal crime or a threat to the national security has or may have
occurred, is or may be occurring, or will or may occur and the
investigation may obtain information relating to the activity or the
involvement or role of an individual, group, or organization in such
activity.

(U) (~~S//NF~~) The ICIG referral provided a sample unclassified e-mail
that allegedly contains information at a classified and SCI level.
According to the ICIG, this e-mail was part of a larger trove of other
unclassified e-mails they were reviewing during their own
investigation.

(U) (~~S//NF~~) The following documentation was provided by the ICIG and
will be kept in the 1A section of the case file.

1) 811 referral letter from the ICIG dated July 6, 2015 regarding
Potential Compromise of Classified Information.
2) Letter from the ICIG dated June 19, 2015 regarding Update to IC
IG support to State Department IG.
3) Letter from the ICIG dated June 25, 2015 regarding Classified
Material on Personal Storage Devices.
4) E-mail dated April 10, 2011 with example of potential inclusion

~~SECRET~~//~~NOFORN~~

2

HRC-349

~~SECRET~~/~~NOFORN~~

Title: (U//~~FOUO~~) Opening of Full Investigation on a Sensitive
Investigative Matter (SIM)
Re: [                    ] 07/10/2015                                    b3
                                                                         b7E

of classified information contained in an unclassified e-mail.
5) Letter from Williams & Connolly LLP dated June 24, 2015 regarding
preservation efforts related to e-mails.

(U)

   (S//NF) Due to the extremely sensitive nature of this
investigation and the damage its disclosure could cause, the case will
be designated as a prohibited investigation in accordance with the
Counterintelligence Division Policy Implementation Guide. Author
requests Assistant Director concurrence to maintain the identified case
as prohibited.

(U) (S//NF) This investigation is also designated a Sensitive
Investigative Matter (SIM) due to a connection to a current public
official, political appointee or candidate as defined in Section
10.1.2.2.2 of the DIOG.

(U) (S//NF) Additionally, an Assistant Director exemption for
uploading to Sentinel is requested. Since the ICIG referral alleges
classified SCI material may have been compromised, all investigative
work will be conducted on SCION. As documents to the case file are
added, a placeholder will be entered into Sentinel and a serial number
assigned to the document. Electronic copies of the case serials will
be stored on SCION. The physical case file documents will be stored in
a locked file cabinet located in [          ] a currently certified SCIF.    b7E

♦♦

~~SECRET~~/~~NOFORN~~

3

HRC-350

have insisted that their sources show them the IGs' alleged criminal referral—or gotten a direct confirmation from the two IGs before posting the story. Of course, hindsight is twenty-twenty. But these were not rookie reporters; they should have known not to rely solely on the late-night confirmations from the Justice Department, or other sources at Justice, including possibly FBI officials who also might have misunderstood the question being asked. Now, the story explained, what they were really trying to confirm was not a criminal referral by the IGs but rather the existence of the July 10 FBI memo that did, in fact, open a criminal investigation of Clinton's emails.

The second important document posted on the FBI's public website was an FBI memo dated July 21, 2015, and hand-delivered on July 23, to Deputy Attorney General Sally Q. Yates, notifying her of that July 10 FBI opening of a criminal investigation of Clinton, noting it was based on the July 6 ICIG "referral." This document, which appears on pages 62–63, was significant because it showed that Justice at the highest levels (including the attorney general) knew that a criminal investigation of Clinton had been initiated by the FBI two weeks before.

So the *Times* and its reporters might ask: Why did the Justice Department withdraw its confirmation of the criminal investigation on July 24 while knowing that two weeks before the FBI had opened a criminal investigation?

The answer is unclear. Perhaps it is because the department faced a dilemma.

Senior Justice officials learned on Friday morning that they had wrongly confirmed on Thursday night that the two IGs had made a criminal referral to the FBI to investigate Clinton. The ICIG publicly stated (and undoubtedly told these top officials sometime that morning) that he had not made a criminal referral to the FBI but rather a "security referral."

But, again, why didn't Justice, after it retracted its confirmation to the *Times*, volunteer that there was, in fact, an open FBI criminal

ALL INFORMATION CONTAINED
HEREIN IS UNCLASSIFIED EXCEPT
WHERE SHOWN OTHERWISE

~~SECRET//NOFORN~~

CLASSIFIED BY: NSICG J37J85T94
REASON: 1.4 (C)
DECLASSIFY ON: 12-31-2040
DATE: 10-27-2016

**U.S. Department of Justice**

Federal Bureau of Investigation

In Reply, Please Refer to
File No.

21 July 2015

To:     Sally Quillian Yates
        Deputy Attorney General
        Department of Justice

From:   Mark F. Giuliano
        Deputy Director
        Federal Bureau of Investigation

(S)

Subject: (~~S//NF~~) [                    ]                                   b1
         MISHANDLING of CLASSIFIED;                                           b3
         UNKNOWN SUBJECT OR COUNTRY;                                          b7E
         SENSITIVE INVESTIGATIVE MATTER (SIM)


(U) (~~S//NF~~) On 13 July 2015 and 20 July 2015, I verbally advised
you of a Section 811(c) referral from the Inspector General of the
Intelligence Community received by the FBI on 06 July 2015.  The
referral addressed the mishandling of classified information on the
personal e-mail account and electronic media of a former high-level
(S) US Government official. On 10 July 2015, the FBI initiated a full      b1
investigation, [                         ] in response to the referral.    b3
Two copies of the opening letterhead memorandum for the investigation      b7E
are attached for the information of the Department of Justice.

(U//~~FOUO~~) The point of contact for this investigation is
Assistant Director Randall C. Coleman, Counterintelligence Division,
telephone number [                    ]                                    b6
                                                                           b7C

*Mark F. Giuliano*

Mark F. Giuliano
FBI, Deputy Director

Derived From:  Multiple Sources
Declassify on 20401231
~~SECRET//NOFORN~~
1                                                          HRC-368

07/21/2015

ALL INFORMATION CONTAINED
HEREIN IS UNCLASSIFIED
DATE 10-27-2016 BY J37J85T94 NSICG

[ ] please have the DD sign these two documents.  One will be provided the DAG/DOJ and the other copy will be placed in our records here at FBIHQ.

b6
b7C

Thanks
Randy

Hand - delivered to DAG
by DD & AD Coleman - 7/23

HRC-369

63

investigation of Clinton as of two weeks before? Most legal experts would agree that they made the right decision not to do so. The long-standing policy of the Justice Department and, indeed, all criminal justice systems in the United States—federal, state, and local—is not to confirm (or deny) the existence of an ongoing criminal investigation. This is based on the principle of due process and the presumption of innocence. To confirm an investigation is to cast a shadow over a citizen who is still supposed to be protected by the due process rights and the presumption of innocence under our Constitution. A person whom the media reports to be under "FBI investigation" is often presumed guilty even before an indictment, much less trial and a verdict—and certainly subject to innuendo of wrongdoing by headlines and partisans, even leading a reckless presidential candidate to lead chants of "Lock her up!" (Ironically, as we shall see in Chapter Six, only James Comey thought that policy and those constitutional principles did not apply to him.)

There was a less important, but still interesting, third document posted: an FBI report of its interview (called a 302) of an inspector in the ICIG's office in Virginia. This document appears on pages 65–67. What made that interview significant is that the second to last paragraph on page 67 confirmed that Clinton's thirty thousand emails were in fact reviewed in two days—June 26–27, 2015. Also, this interview happened to occur on July 23. As we shall see, many of the ICIG and FBI actions adversely affecting Hillary Clinton happened on that day.

These three documents, taken together, raise troubling questions about the judgments and conduct of the FBI and James Comey; the Intelligence Community inspector general, Charles McCullough; and the top management of the Justice Department—questions that can be linked, directly or indirectly, to the decision by Comey on October 28, 2016, to send his letter to Congress.

DECLASSIFIED BY: NSICG  J37J85T94
ON 10-12-2016

FD-302a (Rev. 10-6-95)

SECRET//ORCON//NOFORN

-1-

## FEDERAL BUREAU OF INVESTIGATION

Date of transcription ___07/23/2015___ b3 per ODNI
b6 per FBI
b7C per FBI

(U//FOUO)⬚ date of birth⬚ was interviewed at the Office of the Inspector General of the Intelligence Community, Patriot Park, 12290 Sunrise Valley Drive, Reston, Virginia 20191. Also present during the interview were⬚ and⬚ After being advised of the identity of the interviewing Agents and the nature of the interview,⬚ provided the following information:

b3 per ODNI
b6 per FBI

(U) (S//NF)⬚ had worked as an Inspector in the Office of the Inspector General of the b7C per FBI Intelligence Community (IC/IG) for approximately 2 years. In May 2015, IG/IC began to assist in the Department of State's Inspector General's (STATE/IG) review entitled "Use of Personal Communications Hardware and Software by Five Secretaries of State and Their Immediate Staffs." This assistance was requested pursuant to the March 12, 2015 letter from the United States Senate.

(U) (S//NF) On or about May 28, 2015⬚ met with⬚ the Inspector General, United States Department of State (STATE) and other STATE employees in order to assist in completing the review. It appeared that STATE Freedom of Information Act (FOIA) employees were at least already 6 weeks into the review process.⬚ immediately recognized problems that impeded STATE's review process. Some of the problems were 1) STATE's computer software was at least 2 generations behind; 2) the optical character recognition (OCR) was faulty; and 3) STATE b3 per ODNI b6 per FBI employees used initials to describe organizations, as opposed to using intelligence designations. b7C per FBI ⬚ found STATE FOIA employees very helpful. On various occasions many of the FOIA officials stayed after midnight to conduct the email review.

(U) (S//NF) On or about May 22, 2015, STATE publicly released two hundred ninety-six e-mails belonging to former Secretary of State Hilary Clinton (CLINTON). The two hundred ninety-six e-mails were previously reviewed and released by STATE FOIA officials in response to previous FOIA requests. According to the Defense Intelligence Agency, National Security Agency, and National Geospatial Intelligence Agency officials, at least one of those un-redacted e-mails should have been treated as

| | | | |
|---|---|---|---|
| Investigation on | 07/23/2015 | at | Reston, Virginia |

b3
b7E

File #  ⬚                              Date dictated ___N/A___

By SA⬚

b6
b7C

This document contains neither recommendations nor conclusions of the FBI. It is the property of the FBI and is loaned to your agency; it and its contents are not to be distributed outside your agency.

Classified By: F93M27K51
Derived From: FBI NSIC dated 20130301
Declassify On: 20401231

SECRET//ORCON//NOFORN

HRC-334

65

# The Unmaking of the President 2016

SECRET//ORCON/NOFORN

FD-302a (Rev. 10-6-95)

Continuation of FD-302 of _____ Interview of [REDACTED] _____ , On 07/23/2015 , Page __2__    b3 per ODNI
classified. On or about June 25, 2015 the IC/IG notified the Director of National Intelligence and    b6 per FBI
members of the senate of this leak of classified information.    b7C per FBI

(U) (S//NF)  IC/IG believed that the release of the two hundred ninety-six e-mails did not comply with FOIA regulations. In fact, public figures were completely redacted from the TO, FROM and CC lines, in violation of FOIA regulations. It also appeared that no STATE FOIA personnel knew how the two hundred ninety-six e-mails had been selected to be released. STATE FOIA personnel indicated during the FOIA review process, some B1 (Classified National Security Information) were removed and changed to B5 FOIA exemptions (Privileged Communications). [REDACTED] believed STATE FOIA redactions of    b3 per ODNI
classified information were inappropriately designated or changed.    b6 per FBI
                                                                       b7C per FBI

(U) (S//NF)  The two hundred ninety-six emails were taken from approximately fifty-five thousand pages of thirty thousand e-mails provided to STATE by the Law Offices of Williams & Connolly LLP, (William & Connolly) CLINTON's personal counsel. According to Williams & Connolly, the firm had provided all of CLINTON's work related or potentially work related e-mails from her @clintonemail.com account. Williams & Connolly also maintained a copy of the .PST file containing the electronic copy of the above referenced e-mails, on a thumb drive, stored in a secure safe at Williams & Connolly's Washington, DC office. David Kendall (KENDALL) and Katherine Turner, Esq. (TURNER) were the only two people that had access to the thumb drive. The firm further advised they believed the server equipment used to host CLINTON's @clintonemail.com account was no longer valid or active. Platte River Networks in Colorado maintained custody of the equipment and had received preservation notices.

(U) (S//NF)  IC/IG had considered serving legal process to Williams & Connolly in order to retrieve the thumb drive. Diplomatic Security had attempted to retrieve the thumb drive from William & Connolly, but were informed that since the firm had received preservation letters for the .PST files, the firm could not release the thumb drive to Diplomatic Security. According to [REDACTED] Diplomatic    b3 per ODNI
Security was led to believe Williams & Connolly in fact had 3 copies of the thumb drive.    b6 per FBI
                                                                                            b7C per FBI

(U) (S//NF)  In December 2014, Williams & Connolly informed STATE they had fourteen boxes containing the approximately thirty thousand e-mails. However, when STATE arrived to pick up the boxes, STATE only received twelve boxes. IC/IG had no information as to whether Williams & Connolly were authorized to store classified information or if KENDALL and TURNER held security clearances.

                                                                                   b3 per ODNI
(U) (S//NF) [REDACTED] surmised [REDACTED] and other STATE FOIA officials    b6 per FBI
were suspicious of the special appointments to STATE Legislative Affairs of attorneys [REDACTED]    b7C per FBI
[REDACTED] and [REDACTED] and other STATE FOIA personnel believed the
involvement of [REDACTED] and [REDACTED] in the FOIA review process was abnormal. [REDACTED] and [REDACTED]
made recommendations and requested additional changes that were not routine. [REDACTED] and [REDACTED]
both previously had worked at [REDACTED] which appeared to create a conflict of interest.

SECRET//ORCON/NOFORN

HRC-335

66

SECRET//ORCON/NOFORN

FD-302a (Rev. 10-6-95)

b3 per ODNI
b6 per FBI
b7C per FBI

Continuation of FD-302 of ___ Interview of_____ On 07/23/2015 Page __3__

_____believed both attorneys had also worked at the_____and was possibly involved in the Lois Lerner, Internal Revenue Service situation.

b3 per ODNI
b6 per FBI
b7C per FBI

(U//FOUO) On or about June 15, 2015 IC/IG sent a letter to STATE/IG documenting potential issues identified in the Preliminary Review of the State Department FOIA Process. The recommendations were:

1. Recommend State Department FOIA office request staff support from IC FOIA offices to assist in the identification of intelligence community equities;
2. Recommend IC FOIA officers review the email to ensure that ClassNet use is appropriate before transmitting to the State Bureaus for review;
3. Recommend State Department FOIA seek classification expertise from the interagency to act as a final arbiter if there is a question regarding potentially classified materials;
4. Recommend State Department FOIA Office incorporate the Department of Justice into the FOIA process to ensure the legal sufficiency review of the FOIA exemptions and redactions;

b3 per ODNI
b6 per FBI
b7C per FBI

(U//S//NF) On or about June 26-27, 2015, a review of the thirty thousand e-mails revealed five additional classified e-mails._____used key word searches in order to review the e-mail. It appeared that one in every five e-mail addresses were not a .GOV e-mail address. In the thirty thousand e-mails there were about seventeen unsigned classification upgrade memorandums. These memorandums were packages of information which were being held for the Assistant Secretary of State for Administration's signature.

(U//S//NF) On or about July 1, 2015, IC/IG officials met with Patrick Kennedy, Under Secretary of State for Management and other STATE representatives. IC/IG informed STATE that IC/IG would assist STATE/IG conduct the review, whether or not STATE welcomed IC/IG's input._____alleged STATE made several misrepresentations during this meeting. One such statement made by STATE's legal counsel was "there were no classified information contained in the thirty thousand e-mails".

b3 per ODNI
b6 per FBI
b7C per FBI

_____was willing to assist the FBI further as needed.

b3 per ODNI
b6 per FBI
b7C per FBI

SECRET//ORCON/NOFORN

HRC-336

\* \* \*

But first let's go back to July 10, 2015—the memo opening the FBI criminal investigation that was not public, that no one in the media knew about at the time and never had a chance to read until it was posted on January 8, 2017—two months after the election—on the FBI's public "vault." A close reading of that secret FBI July 10 memo reveals that the Bureau's decision to open a criminal investigation was based on facts in part allegedly "provided" in ICIG McCullough's July 6 "referral," which raises the first question about that decision: How can the FBI justify opening a criminal investigation based on what the ICIG stated when, two weeks later, on July 24, the ICIG publicly stated its referral was "not criminal"?

The memo is from "FBIHQ, Counterespionage Section," the Bureau's headquarters in Washington. This means that FBI director James Comey himself presumably authorized the opening of this criminal investigation of Hillary Clinton. (Although her name is redacted from the memo, there are many indications that she is the subject, such as the fact that the investigation was designated as a "Sensitive Investigative Matter due to a connection to a current public official, political appointee or candidate . . .") That is another reason why it is safe to assume that James Comey as director likely personally approved the opening of this investigation.

The first page of the memo states the synopsis of the investigation: "FBIHQ, Counterespionage Section, is opening a full investigation based on specific articulated facts provided by an 811 referral from the Inspector General of the Intelligence Community, dated July 6, 2015 regarding the potential compromise of classified information."

Section 811 of the Intelligence Authorization Act of 1995 allows an executive branch officer, such as the ICIG, to advise the FBI of any information that "indicates that classified information . . . may have been disclosed in an unauthorized manner to a foreign power or agent of a foreign power." It does not necessarily involve a criminal investigation. Often an 811 referral from a department to the FBI merely advises the need for a review by the FBI's noncriminal counterintelligence division experts to determine whether unmarked documents requested under the Freedom of Information Act should be marked "classified" and, thus, withheld from disclosure. As the *Los Angeles Times* reported, Section 811 referrals from the ICIG "may or may not ultimately launch an investigation. Experts say such referrals from an intelligence agency inspector general are routine and often do not lead to much."[1]

This is what a source close to McCullough described as McCullough's understanding of the document he sent to the FBI on July 6, 2015: When he sent his July 6 "referral" to the FBI, it was not necessarily about initiating a criminal case. Rather, he sent his referral to the FBI as a notice under Section 811 for "counterintelligence purposes." What he meant by that was summarized in the July 23, 2015, memo, which he has said to the source was virtually identical to the July 23 memo to Congress that was made public the next day, on July 24, after the *New York Times* story ran.

McCullough's referral, the source said, was intended to seek support from the FBI to pressure State to allow representatives of the Intelligence Community, as well as the Counterintelligence Division of the FBI, to participate in State's ongoing FOIA review process of Hillary Clinton's emails. McCullough expressed concerns in that July 6 referral (and the July 23 memo) that the State Department had rejected requests for such participation in that FOIA review process by representatives from the Intel Community and FBI counterintelligence experts. The source said that McCullough never intended his submission to the FBI on July 5 to be characterized as a "criminal referral," because it was not.

There are specific rules governing when the FBI is allowed to open a criminal investigation. They are contained in the *Domestic Investigations*

*and Operations Guide (DIOG or FBI Operations Guide). DIOG* Section
7.5 states that to open a full criminal investigation, the FBI must have
a specific "articulable factual basis" that "reasonably indicates . . . an
activity constituting a federal crime or threat to the national security
has or may have occurred."

The FBI memo includes on page 2 only a single fact to satisfy its
criterion of a specific "articulable factual basis" for the belief that
Clinton may have committed a crime "regarding the potential compromise of classified information": ". . . a sample unclassified e-mail
that allegedly contains information at a classified and SCI [Sensitive
Compartmented Information] level. According to the ICIG, this
e-mail was part of a larger trove of other unclassified e-mails they
were reviewing during their own investigation."

However, this single fact cannot possibly satisfy the *Operations
Guide* criteria as stated. While this single email allegedly contained
information at a classified and SCI level, that does not establish that
a crime may have been committed because neither ICIG McCullough
nor the FBI in this memo stated the email in question had appropriate classified markings. And we know that without such classified
markings, Secretary Clinton could not be said even "possibly" to have
committed a crime, because, in the absence of the secretary ignoring
emails that were appropriately marked as classified, the FBI had no
basis for finding that she had criminal intent. How do we know this?
Because Comey himself said so, on July 5, 2016, when he announced
that no reasonable prosecutor could bring a criminal case against
Clinton for her email practices.

These rules do not allow a criminal investigation to be opened
based on a "hunch" that there "possibly" could be marked emails
if the FBI looked at all thirty thousand Clinton emails. Indeed, the
words of Section 7.5 of the FBI's *Operations Guide* require a "specific,
articulable fact" to be possessed by the FBI *first*—suggesting the
possibility a crime has been committed before a criminal investi-

gation can be opened—*not after* the criminal investigation has been opened, so that FBI agents can go on a fishing expedition in search of predicate facts.

So, since there were no emails properly marked as classified that could serve as predicate facts, what did the FBI include in its July 10, 2015, memo as "predicate facts" to justify opening the criminal investigation under Section 7.5's standards? The memo referred to five documents. However, not one of the five cited a marked Clinton email—or any other known predicate facts that could possibly lead to a criminal prosecution.

The first document cited in the July 10 secret FBI memo was McCullough's July 6 ICIG "referral." Significantly, the FBI header for the July 6 referral was "Potential Compromise of Classified Information." "Potential" is not a fact. To make it a fact requires a search for a fact. That conflicts with the requirements of Section 7.5. Moreover, just consider: The FBI was using the McCullough July 6 referral as a basis for opening a criminal investigation. Yet, two weeks later—on July 24—McCullough himself publicly announced that the document he sent to the FBI was "not" a criminal referral but a noncriminal "security referral"—meaning for counterintelligence purposes to prevent classified information from being disclosed under FOIA requests.

Looking more closely at McCullough's July 23, 2015, memo sent to Congress two weeks after his "referral" to the FBI, it can be seen there were only two facts asserted in the entire memo. (See page 34.)

First: "We note that none of the emails we reviewed had classification or dissemination markings, but some included IC-derived classified information and should have been handled as classified, appropriately marked, and transmitted via a secure network. Further, my office's limited sampling of 40 of the emails revealed four contained IC information which should have been marked and handled at the SECRET level."

This couldn't be clearer: McCullough stated that "none" of the emails reviewed by his office had classified markings; thus there could never have been criminal intent found regarding Secretary Clinton, as Comey announced a year later on July 5. McCullough's statement that some of these emails "should have" been marked was, as he stated, for the purpose of withholding them from FOIA disclosure. But "should have" is not a predicate fact that could be the basis of a criminal prosecution.

The second fact asserted by McCullough was: "The 30,000 emails in question are purported to have been copied to a thumb drive in the possession of former Secretary Clinton's personal counsel, Williams and Connelly [*sic*] attorney David Kendall."

This fact cannot possibly constitute a factual predicate for opening a criminal investigation of Secretary Clinton. The transfer of these emails to Clinton's attorney on a private thumb drive, kept under lock and key in Kendall's law offices, cannot possibly be the basis of a criminal investigation. As we know, a year later, the FBI never suggested, nor did Comey on July 5 even mention, such transfer from Clinton to her personal attorney under conditions of strict security.

In sum: There is not a single specific articulable fact that the FBI cited in its July 10 memo based on what ICIG McCullough stated in his July 6, 2015, noncriminal referral to the FBI, or any other fact independently cited by the FBI in the memo, that meets the standard of Section 7.5 of the FBI's *Operations Guide*. It appears that from the beginning the FBI never had the "predicate fact" required for them to initiate the full criminal investigation of Hillary Clinton, according to their own rules. And a year later, Comey confirmed that there was no crime possible, with the requisite criminal intent, in the absence of emails that were appropriately marked as classified.

This could be the explanation why, at that same time, Comey

said that the FBI had found a "small number" of emails that had a portion with classified markings but then two days later was forced to take that back late in the day at a public congressional hearing. That retraction or modification of his July 5 statement was little noted in the media—a tree falling in the forest. And of course, no one in the media at that point knew about the secret July 10, 2015, memo opening the criminal investigation and that the memo stated no predicate facts or identified no Clinton marked emails in violation of the Bureau's Section 7.5 of its *Operations Guide*.

Even if the FBI claims that it had a reasonable suspicion it would find marked Clinton emails if it took more time to find them, including a few thousand that seemed not to have been transferred to her private server from her BlackBerry in her first few months as secretary, why did it take Comey and the FBI a full year to complete the investigation? In fact, it could have taken no more than two days to review all thirty thousand of Clinton's State Department–related emails to determine whether any had classified markings. How do we know this? As already noted above, in the FBI's interview of an ICIG inspector on July 23, 2015, the third document referenced above, the inspector is quoted as saying that on June 26–27, 2015, a review of all the thirty thousand emails was completed. That's right: two days to inspect thirty thousand emails. A source close to McCullough claimed that this review was cursory and the ICIG inspector was "kicked out" after two days. Even if that is true, the State Department would not have refused to allow FBI agents in the middle of a criminal investigation full access for as long as they needed to confirm that not one of those thirty thousand emails was appropriately marked as classified. So why didn't the FBI just go to State and ask to review Clinton's emails?

What would have happened if Comey had done this and announced on October 5, 2015—or December 5, for that matter, five months after the fact—that there was no prosecutable case against Clinton, rather than waiting until the following July? We will never know.

\*    \*    \*

Meanwhile, once the July 10, 2015, secret decision to open the criminal investigation had been made, the FBI senior leadership wanted to be certain that the number-two official of the Justice Department, Deputy Attorney General (DAG) Sally Q. Yates, knew about it. That doesn't seem unusual. But it seemed that they wanted to be very, very certain she knew—especially certain that she knew on July 23.

So they notified her verbally on July 13.

They notified her a second time verbally, on July 20, just in case she hadn't heard the first time that the FBI had opened an investigation of the front-running Democratic presidential candidate.

Then to be *absolutely sure* DAG Yates understood after two verbal notifications, they wrote her a memo stating the same, dated July 21.

Then to be *absolutely positively sure* that she had received the memo, on—guess what date?—July 23, 2015, Deputy Director Mark Giuliano and the assistant director, Counterintelligence Division, Randall C. Coleman, *hand-delivered* the letter to Yates. How do we know this? Because of a handwritten note someone scrawled at the bottom of the second page, under the signature line: "Hand-delivered to DAG by DD [Deputy Director Giuliano] & AD [Assistant Director Coleman]" and then "7/23." This is a very conscientious effort by senior management of the FBI.

Concerning the role played by the Intelligence Community inspector general, Charles McCullough, according to a source close to him, he was increasingly frustrated that the State Department resisted allowing his Intel Community colleagues to help in the review process of the Clinton emails. He claims that had he been allowed to do so, he would not have sent the same kind of referral to the FBI, complaining about the State Department's noncooperation and resistance to allowing the Intel Community to be involved in the FOIA review process. His referral, his source says, to the FBI would have been more benign, more in the nature of a notice, "we are all working well together." He even speculated, according to the source, that he might not have needed to send any referral to the FBI had there been full participation by the IC classification experts, the FBI counterintelligence experts, and the State Department. In such an event, he says, he would not have needed to use the language he used in his July 23 memo, warning that classified information that "should have been" marked might be released under FOIA, and Intelligence Community experts needed to be involved in the State Department FOIA review process.

McCullough also insisted, through this source, that he was not making judgments about the existence of classified information. He was passing along the judgments of experts in the Intelligence Community, he said. McCullough's explanation remains suspect. He worked as a senior FBI official in the 1990s under the then openly anti–President Clinton FBI director, Louis Freeh.

And he could hardly credibly claim to be "shocked, shocked" by the leaks of his anti-Clinton memos from a Republican-led congressional committee. It is a simple fact that State Department officials had plenty of reason to doubt that McCullough and some members of the Intelligence Community were neutral arbiters in reviewing Clinton's emails. Their history of overclassifying was a reality in Washington and well known. The best example remained their insistence that a Clinton email forwarding a published article about U.S. drones being used in Pakistan's Tribal Areas was classified information. Why should State classification experts trust that given their tendency to overclassify, inviting in Intelligence Community officials would not just lead to protracted debates and inevitable leaks to Republican partisans in Congress, who would then leak to the media?

In any event, even had McCullough not sent any referral to the FBI on July 6 or a benign one, signs suggest that the FBI and Comey would have found another reason to open a criminal investigation. As it was, they had no predicate facts—no Clinton emails marked classified—and yet they secretly began the criminal investigation as set forth in their secret July 10, 2015, memo. They seemed determined to open the investigation regardless of their own rules, as the memo shows.

As it turned out, the tensions between McCullough and the State Department continued and got worse through the rest of 2015, and McCullough's continued concerns about classified information getting into the public domain—that is, what he believed to be classified information—undoubtedly continued to infect the attitude of the FBI that there was something being concealed by the Clinton camp, particularly on the hard drive or in deleted emails that needed to be part of a criminal investigation.

For example, on January 19, 2016, the *Hill* newspaper reported that it had obtained a letter—"first reported by Fox News"—that McCullough had written to Congress stating that among Clinton's emails stored on her server was "highly classified information known as 'special access programs' (SAP)." The McClatchy newspaper chain reported the next day that McCullough had written a letter to two Republican senators saying that "several dozen" emails Clinton sent and received while she was secretary of state contained "classified material at the highest levels."

McCullough, according to the source close to him, became defensive about the charges that were made about him as anti-Clinton or making stretched judgments about what was classified information. "I was just a conduit for the judgments of others in the Intel Community," he told his source. But his insistence that he sent his information to congressional oversight committees chaired by partisan Republicans without understanding they would be used for partisan purposes against Hillary Clinton—or, more accurately, misused and mischaracterized—or leaked to the media is at best naïve, and is difficult for Washington veterans on both sides of the aisle to believe.

Brian Fallon unsurprisingly commented to CNN about the McCullough-to-Congress-to-the-media pattern of leaks: "I think this is a very coordinated leak."

This wasn't just a complaint from the Clinton campaign. On March 5, 2016, seven congressional Democrats—four Democratic ranking U.S. senators and three members of the House Intelligence, Foreign Affairs, and Government Oversight Committees—wrote a letter to both ICIG McCullough and State's IG Linick, expressing concerns that the offices of both IGs were not conducting their reviews of Clinton's emails appropriately. The seven Democrats referenced "errors and transgressions in misclassifying" documents that turned out not to contain any classified information at all, information shared with just Republican members of Congress and not Democrats, and briefing journalists in a way that was "not transparent and neutral."[2]

IG Linick subsequently conducted a review of email practices of four previous secretaries of state and issued a report as a result of that review on May 26, 2016. While the media focused its headlines on the critique of Clinton using a private email system and waiting two years to turn over all her official business emails, downplayed was the fact that Linick had found general problems of explaining and enforcing policy and rules on using private email systems by the State Department going back many administrations. Linick also disclosed that former secretary of state General Colin Powell also used a private email system outside the State Department server, on AOL.

In this story on the State IG's report, the media showed its tendency to blow up critical evaluations of Clinton and ignore ones that mitigated the criticism as it had throughout the reporting of the Clinton email story. A typical example was the *Washington Post* headline "State Department Slams Clinton Over Emails."*[3]

Let us now ask whether Deputy Attorney General Yates, who had supervisory authority over Comey and the FBI in any criminal investigation of Hillary Clinton (since Attorney General Loretta Lynch had recused herself after Bill Clinton's June 27 visit with her on the tarmac at Phoenix International Airport), exercised any oversight at all.

As we now know, Yates had been informed by a hand-delivered letter on July 21 from the deputy director of the FBI that the FBI had received a July 6 referral from ICIG McCullough and had opened a full criminal investigation, as memorialized in a memo four days later, on July 10. Indeed, the letter from the FBI stated she had been verbally notified two times of the Clinton email criminal investigation.

Little is known about what Yates did when she learned about that secret July 10 memo and the criminal investigation of Clinton.

Did Yates ask to read the secret July 10 memo? Did she ask to see the "specific articulable predicate facts" required under FBI rules to open that investigation? At least by July 24, Yates knew that McCullough had contradicted the *New York Times* report that he had made a criminal referral to the FBI. Did she ever question Comey as to his basis for opening a criminal investigation? In other words, did Deputy Attorney General Yates exercise, prudently and responsibly, her supervisory authority over Comey and the FBI? Did she make it crystal clear to Comey that he reported to her and that, while she would not compromise the independence and thoroughness of his

* A full reading of the report challenges the *Post*'s decision to use the hyperbole "slams" in the headline—as did most other mainstream media reports—while omitting the mitigating findings that the department for many years had failed to articulate clear and coherent policy and rules on private emails.

investigation, she expected it to be high priority and expedited as much as possible?

If the deputy attorney general did not ask any of these questions, and did not convey to Comey clearly that he was subject to her supervision and accountability, that would have been a very bad omen for Hillary Clinton.

# PART II

# The Dangers of a Righteous Man

# CHAPTER FIVE

# Policy and Fairness Be Damned

On July 5, 2016, after nearly a year of an extensive investigation by the FBI's Counterintelligence Division, involving hundreds of agents mostly out of DC headquarters, James Comey decided to hold a press conference to announce the findings.

The news was very positive for Hillary Clinton. Here is the headline that *should have* dominated coverage over the next days, accurately describing the contents of Comey's 2,314-word statement, read to a huge international TV audience: "FBI Director Comey Recommends No Prosecution of Clinton over Emails Practices; Finds No Intent to Violate Law, No Emails Marked Classified; No Evidence Private Server Hacked."

This fictional headline accurately reflects what James Comey concluded. It should have been the end of the media's preoccupation with emails, and Hillary Clinton's poll numbers should have significantly improved.

But instead, almost all the media reaction was negative and Clinton's standing went *down*. If anything, the media's obsession with her emails increased. Negativity increased. Donald Trump continued to lead cheers of "Lock her up!"

Why did this happen? How could such a positive outcome result in such negative political consequences for Clinton? And how could the media be so complicit?

The answer is not complicated; it's a combination of two factors. First, Comey's statement downplayed the positive findings and repeatedly qualified them with such words as "possible" or "potential" in referring to wrongdoing. For example, it wasn't until the thirty-second paragraph out of a total of thirty-seven that he stated his conclusion that no reasonable criminal case could be brought against Clinton. You had to read and reread the statement to recognize that Comey had *validated* Clinton's repeated insistence that she had never sent or received emails marked classified. And therefore, in the absence of classified emails, there was no evidence of criminal intent. Moreover, even when he articulated positive conclusions about Clinton's conduct, such as that no prosecution was justified and no hacking had been detected despite extensive FBI forensic investigations, he qualified those factual findings with the reminder that there could have been "potential" violations or "possible" hacking.

Let's examine exactly what Comey said—and then how he spun the positives into negatives with innuendo, and with a compliant mainstream media following suit.

> Although there is evidence of potential violations of the statutes regarding the handling of classified information, . . . no reasonable prosecutor would bring such a case. . . . No charges are appropriate . . .

As noted, "no reasonable prosecutor . . . " is the heart of the news that everyone in the Clinton camp had been waiting for after a year-long FBI investigation. Comey could have started and stopped there, perhaps adding a single sentence of explanation: After reviewing the more than thirty-three thousand\* Clinton emails, he and his FBI team could find none with "recognizable" classified markings as required by the classification manual.

Instead, Comey preceded this positive conclusion for Clinton with the qualifier "although" and with "*potential* violations of the statutes . . ." You don't have to be a lawyer or even a defender of Hillary Clinton to wonder about the propriety of the director of the FBI publicly using the word "potential" in this situation.

Why did Comey do this? It is hard to resist seeing this as an effort to balance his positive conclusions with red meat rhetoric aimed at Republican critics, who were likely to be upset by his no-prosecution recommendation. It arguably appears to represent bias: stating good facts and conclusions for Clinton . . . and then undermining them with innuendo and weasel words that suggest wrongdoing.

Comey explained why he said no reasonable prosecutor would bring a case against Clinton by comparing Clinton's case with others that had been brought under the Espionage Act for mishandling of classified information. He continued:

> In looking back at our investigations into mishandling or removal of classified information, we cannot find a case that would support bringing criminal charges on these facts [applicable to Secretary Clinton's conduct]. All the cases prosecuted involved some combination of clearly intentional and willful mishandling of classified information; or vast quantities of materials exposed in such a way as to support an inference of intentional misconduct and willful

\* The number thirty-three thousand is used here, rather than the usual number—approximately thirty thousand—of State Department–related emails turned over by Clinton in December 2014. This is because in his statement, Comey mentioned "several thousand" additional emails recovered by the FBI and inadvertently not included in the original total. I have estimated "several thousand" to mean about three thousand.

mishandling of classified information; or vast quantities of materials exposed in such a way as to support an inference of intentional misconduct; or indications of disloyalty.

In other words, Clinton did none of these things—nothing intentionally or willfully. And given the absence of classified markings on the emails, that conclusion was inevitable. This arguably meant the FBI investigation had been a rabbit hole from the start. It just took $20 million and a full year to reach that conclusion.

Comey concluded that no case could be brought against Clinton because FBI agents were unable to identify emails marked as classified. As noted, that was true when the FBI opened its criminal investigation of Clinton. Twelve months later, he could still not cite a single email that had recognizable classified markings among the thirty-three thousand reviewed.

But then Comey added a misleading and harmful assertion. He stated that contrary to Clinton's many prior statements throughout the campaign that she had never sent or received emails marked as classified, the FBI had, in fact, found a "small number" of marked emails that Clinton had "sent or received" that contained information with classified markings—in effect accusing Clinton of making false statements. But a close reading of the words Comey chose to use in the July 5 statement suggested that he was not being entirely forthcoming. Here is what Comey said: "It is important to say something about the marking of classified information. Only a *very small number* of the emails containing classified information *bore markings indicating the presence of classified information*" (emphasis added).

Strange wording. Seemed intentionally vague, incomplete. Why didn't he just say a very few number of emails were "marked classified" instead of "indicated the presence of . . ."? Why use such circuitous language? Why "very few"? Why not state the actual number?

The mystery would be resolved two days later at a congressional hearing when Comey was forced to modify and then withdraw his claim under questioning from a Democratic congressman. But not before the damaging headlines across the country's mainstream media, on TV and the Internet, that Comey had "accused" Clinton of "lying" because she had claimed never to have received any emails with "classified markings" or "identified as classified."

On July 7, Comey testified before the House Oversight Committee to answer questions about his July 5 public statement. The day before that testimony, the media reported that Comey's phrase a "very small number" of emails was only three emails. Then we learned from the State Department that the actual number Comey was referring to was a single email, not three.

Then, under questioning at the House Oversight Committee hearings on July 7, Comey was forced to retract his claim that even this single email out of thirty-three thousand bore "markings" that could be recognized as designating classification status of a "portion" of the email.

But first Comey was questioned by the highly partisan, anti-Clinton congressman Trey Gowdy (R-SC), who had led the Benghazi investigation of Clinton that landed no serious blows on her after eleven hours of testimony on national TV. Gowdy asked Comey during the early part of that day's testimony: "Secretary Clinton said there was nothing marked classified on her emails either sent or received. Was that true?"

Comey responded, "That's not true. There were a small number of portion markings on, I think, three of the documents."

The term "portion markings" in and of itself is misleading. If a document contains classified information within a section that also contains nonclassified information, it can be "portion-marked." But the *Intelligence Community Manual* has strict requirements for those markings—how they should be written and made conspicuous within the text.

Not long after Gowdy's misleading question and Comey's misleading answer, Rep. Matt Cartwright (D-PA) smoked out the truth. Here is the transcript:

CARTWRIGHT: All right. You were asked about markings on a few documents. I have the manual here, marking classified national security information. And I don't think you were given a full chance to talk about those three documents with the little "c"s on them. Were they properly documented? Were they properly marked according to the manual?

COMEY: No.

CARTWRIGHT: According to the manual, and I ask unanimous consent to enter this into the record, Mr. Chairman.

[REP. JASON] CHAFFETZ: Without objection . . .

CARTWRIGHT: According to the manual, if you're going to classify something, there has to be a header on the document. Right?

COMEY: Correct.

CARTWRIGHT: Was there a header on the three documents that we've discussed today that had the little "c" in the text someplace?

COMEY: No. There were three e-mails, the "c" was in the body, in the text, but there was no header on the emails or in the text.

CARTWRIGHT: So if Secretary Clinton really were an expert at what's classified and what's not classified and were following the manual, the absence of a header would tell her immediately that those three documents were not classified. Am I correct in that?

COMEY: That would be a reasonable inference.

So here we have Comey omitting the essential fact that only a little "c" in the middle of three (actually, as it turned out, just one) emails was supposed to be noticed by Clinton as identifying "classified information." And that little "c" justified all the headlines that Clinton had "lied." Obviously, if it would be "a reasonable inference" that an expert would not recognize that little "c" as identifying classified information, neither should Hillary Clinton be expected to. Nor did he add that, absent this single instance of a little "c," Clinton had told the truth that none of the emails she sent or received were marked classified. And all the media's headlines and Republican charges that Clinton had "lied" when repeatedly making that statement were now wrong.

Clearly, Comey and the leaders of the FBI's investigation knew that the little "c" did not comply with the detailed, mandatory requirements of classified markings outlined in the *Intelligence Community Manual*, down to punctuation marks and the requirements of headers and footers, with precise wording and rules.* Their use of this obscure wording—"a very small" number of emails that "bore markings indicating the presence of classified information"—seems suspect. Were they trying to avoid admitting that they had initiated the criminal investigation the year before lacking the single "specific articulable fact," i.e., an email that was clearly marked classified, that their own regulations required before a full criminal investigation could be opened?

Comey was not the only hypocrite when it came to dealing with his own admission before Congressman Cartwright. Almost every mainstream media organization—print, network news, cable, websites—

---

* The *Intelligence Community and Control Markings Implementation Manual* is a 160-page document that describes in excruciating detail how to mark documents that contain classified information—especially the need for conspicuous banners, specific punctuation, font size, slash marks, levels of classification with different requirements, syntax, etc. For example, "Classification and control markings shall be applied explicitly and uniformly when creating, disseminating, and using classified and unclassified information. . . . The banner line must be conspicuously placed at the top and bottom (header and footer) of each page, in a way that clearly distinguishes it from the informational text . . ." You get the idea.

failed to report that passage of his statement accurately, and then, after his modification on July 7, failed to correct their prior reporting that Clinton had "lied."

In the end, the most harmful negative expression used by Comey in his July 5 public statement announcing his no-prosecution recommendation was when Comey expressed his opinion that Hillary Clinton's conduct in handling unmarked emails was "extremely careless."

Let's be clear: It is simply wrong for a prosecutor, much less a criminal investigator, whether he or she is the FBI director or a detective in a local police department, to publicly express a disparaging opinion of someone who has been the subject of a criminal investigation and not do so within a public charging document, such as an indictment or "information" filed with the court. To do so threatens both due process rights and the presumption of innocence.

Instead, the headlines about Comey's description of Clinton as "extremely careless" were repeated over and over again, and all the offsetting and mitigating facts just mentioned were omitted by almost all the media. Indeed, Comey's "extremely careless" opinion was repeated so many times in so many media venues that by sheer repetition alone it seemed to morph from subjective opinion into eternal fact. Even the Clinton campaign gave up trying to contest the statement.

The attack by partisan Republicans focused on Comey's "extremely careless" opinion and contended, without any evidence, that Hillary Clinton put national security at risk by transferring "classified" emails onto her private server, which could have been hacked by America's enemies. Some of the more reckless even used the word "treasonous" to describe her actions.

However, such critics seemed angry and disbelieving when Comey announced that the FBI's technical experts who had searched Clinton's private server and hard drive found no evidence it had been hacked or compromised.

This was a very good news headline for Clinton. But as was apparent, Comey was not satisfied leaving a positive Clinton fact unqualified by some negative innuendo. So he added that it was "possible" that "hostile actors" had managed to breach Clinton's server without leaving any evidence. So again, Comey's claim that he was apolitical and acting only in the spirit of transparency is refuted. His bias, intentional or not, is apparent.

The public reaction to Comey's July 5 press conference was quite negative. Clinton's personal standings in the favorable versus unfavorable opinion polling that followed the Comey statements dropped considerably.

Ever since the 2015 *Times* stories on Clinton's emails, voters' negative impression of her had consistently exceeded their positive impression. However, in the winter and spring of 2015–2016, as Clinton was winning impressive victories to lock up the Democratic nomination, her unfavorables in national polling data started to drop and her favorables began to increase. For example, in the well-respected Reuters/Ipsos poll taken between June 25 and 29, 2016, with a relatively large sample of 1,247 registered voters nationwide, Clinton showed only a net -8 percent of unfavorable impressions (54 percent unfavorable versus 46 percent favorable), one of her smallest net minus numbers for some time. In a poll taken a week later, between July 2 and 6, Reuters/Ipsos showed a similar result with an entirely different sample of 1,345 registered voters nationwide—a net unfavorable of -10 percent, in this case 55 percent unfavorable, 45 percent favorable opinions.

After the July 5 news went out that Comey had recommended against criminal prosecution, the Clinton campaign expected positive results in the media and in the polls and a virtual end to the email issue as a cloud over the campaign. But the reverse happened.

From that 10 percent net negative ending on July 6 to the very first poll taken after Comey's press conference, spanning July 5 to 9, the results showed an immediate significant negative impact on Clinton's personal standing. A McClatchy-Marist poll of 1,249 adults showed that Clinton's net unfavorable impressions margin over favorables had shot up to 25 percent. Specifically, Clinton's unfavorables went from 55 percent to 60 percent, and her favorables declined from 45 percent to 35 percent. Three other polls with different national samples taken at the same time showed virtually identical results.

This negative public opinion of Clinton was not matched by a negative opinion of Comey for violating Justice Department policies and fundamental principles of fairness when he offered his personal opinion of evidence even as he did not recommend bringing charges.

Among professionals though—regardless of party, administration, or whether they were current or former prosecutors, legal experts—the verdict is that James Comey violated long-standing Justice Department policies and principles of due process by his actions.

Bethany McLean wrote in a February 2017 *Vanity Fair* article, "Comey, according to his critics, compounded his mistake [in holding the press conference in the first place] by declaring Clinton's conduct and that of her aides 'extremely careless.' This was another breach of protocol. Neither prosecutors nor agents criticize people they don't charge."

"We don't dirty you up," Richard Frankel, a former FBI agent who retired in 2016, told *Vanity Fair*.

McLean wrote that "plenty of Comey's longtime admirers were appalled he had spoken at all, because by doing so he blew through several of the Justice Department's long-standing policies." And here was the judgment about Comey spoken by a former prosecutor who once worked for him: "It was an unprecedented public announcement by a non-prosecutor that there would be no prosecution." The FBI does not talk publicly about its investigations and "it does not make prosecutorial decisions. Full stop."

What happens if the policies are ignored? What is the danger? Elizabeth Drew, in the *New York Review of Books* on November 3, 2016, wrote about Comey's willingness to express his "extremely careless" opinion:

> By doing something prosecutors simply don't do, Comey set a dangerous precedent. Any number of prosecutors might conclude later if it was ok for the FBI director to damage the reputation of a person who had just been let off without prosecution (or in Clinton's case damage it further), they could feel free to follow suit. Anyone who wasn't troubled by Comey's performance wasn't thinking through its implications. One could only conclude that his comments were meant for various audiences not in the room: the Republican-dominated Congress and conservative Hillary-haters among the commentariat, and discontented FBI agents who'd wanted him to rule the other way.

Jeffrey Toobin, a former federal prosecutor, agreed in a prescient August 2015 commentary in the *New Yorker*:

> The consequences for Clinton [of being accused of mishandling classified emails] . . . are far more likely to be political than legal. Criminal violations for mishandling classified information all have intent requirements; in other words, to be guilty of a crime, there must be evidence that Clinton knew that the information was classified and intentionally disclosed it to an unauthorized person.

There is no evidence she did anything like that. This is not now a criminal matter, and there is no realistic possibility it will turn into one. (Clinton's critics have noted that General David Petraeus pleaded guilty to a misdemeanor in connection with the disclosure of classified information to his biographer. But Petraeus acknowledged both that he knew the information was classified and that his biographer was not cleared to receive it. Because Clinton said that she did not believe the information was classified, and because she turned it over to cleared State Department employees, the comparison is inapt.)

Comey's violation of long-standing policies is beyond dispute. A man who seemed to sincerely believe he was above politics and would never allow politics to affect his judgment appeared to go out of his way to include in his statement negative innuendo and suppositions to provide some immunity from Republican criticism.

Who was supervising Comey? Where were the attorney general and deputy attorney general to whom Comey and the FBI were legally accountable? Was the July 5, 2016, press conference now the second instance, after his 2015 announcement of an FBI investigation, of an ominous pattern, in which the attorney general and the deputy attorney general appeared to fear the political consequences of supervising Comey and requiring him to follow DOJ policies?

One place from which to begin an answer to that question is Phoenix Airport, where on Monday, June 26, 2016, in the late afternoon, former president Bill Clinton was ready to depart on his private plane parked on the tarmac when he noticed that Attorney General Loretta Lynch's plane was parked next to his. He was an admirer of Lynch and her career as a tough top prosecutor in Brooklyn and as the first African American female to lead the Justice Department. So he decided to pay her a quick social visit. Accounts have it that she felt awkward about saying no, but awkward in the context of an FBI investigation of his wife about saying yes. She agreed to allow him on her plane for a quick hello. The visit lasted about twenty minutes. According to both, they talked only about personal things—children, golf, grandchildren. And that was all.

Nevertheless, Attorney General Lynch was aware of the bad political optics. Republicans suggested that she had to recuse herself from any role in supervising the FBI investigation of Secretary Clinton. So the next day, she said she would accept the FBI's recommendations on whether or not to prosecute Hillary Clinton.

She didn't need to do that, according to many former Justice Department officials, including former attorneys general, but she did. In any event, Lynch never explained why she did not openly deputize Deputy Attorney General Sally Yates to supervise and provide oversight for FBI director Comey's decisions to go public regarding the Clinton investigation.

Moreover, the attorney general did not, nor could she, remove herself from overall responsibilities to enforce long-standing policies of the Justice Department, and to fulfill her obligations to enforce constitutional safeguards in the law enforcement process over which she presided for the entire federal government—especially every citizen's right to due process of law and the presumption of innocence. Those policies and those constitutional safeguards applied to everyone at Justice, from junior prosecutors in the offices of the ninety-three United States attorneys in the country to every department prosecutor and investigator, including every FBI agent and Director James Comey. And of course, Sally Yates had those oversight responsibilities as well.

By his own words at the opening of his July 5 press conference, Comey expressed his independence from oversight by the attorney general and deputy attorney general—in fact, "open defiance" might describe his attitude. He said, "I have not coordinated or reviewed this statement in any way with the Department of Justice or any other part of the government. They do not know what I am about to say."

When J. Edgar Hoover in the 1940s and 1950s established the FBI and himself as an unaccountable power unto themselves, not subject to supervision by the Justice Department or even, it seemed, the president of the United States, most people then attributed and historians now attribute the rogue Hoover's power to his possessing personal files that he used to threaten anyone who might challenge his independence and lack of accountability, including presidents of the United States. But once Hoover was gone, the view among future presidents and students of the Justice Department and the rule of law was: Never again would we allow an FBI director to have such power, to be so unaccountable. In 1968 and 1976, federal laws were changed, giving the FBI director a fixed term of ten years and reconfirming that the FBI and its director were part of the Department of Justice and the director was accountable as a direct report to the attorney general and the deputy attorney general, and could be terminated with cause by the president of the United States before the end of his or her ten-year term.

Yet, there is no indication that Deputy Attorney General Sally Q. Yates (who was now Comey's supervisor after Attorney General Lynch had recused herself following the Clinton tarmac visit) attempted to exercise any meaningful control on Comey, even after he exhibited his clear willingness to act contrary to department policy. Certainly she does not appear to have warned him against testifying before Congress and saying more than simply repeating and explaining his decision not to recommend prosecution of Clinton or told him to avoid any further offering of opinions and evaluations of the evidence concerning Clinton's email practices.

A former senior Justice Department official close to Yates explained why Yates did not call in Comey after his July 5 press conference and challenge his statement that he had intentionally not informed the attorney general or the DAG about holding the press conference or the contents of his statement. This was, the source said, a pragmatic decision. There was concern, based on Comey's past history, that he might leak such a challenge by Yates to the media, through "friends and associates," as an effort to muzzle him or to thwart his ability to investigate Clinton. Therefore, the judgment among senior Justice officials, Yates included, was: What's done is done, and best to leave Comey alone. Why risk a Comey-instigated political firestorm, the source asked, when everyone believed there was no chance Donald Trump was going to win? So the message conveyed to Comey, with no one challenging what he did on July 5 and what he said, must have been: *You are on your own—you will have no serious supervision by the Justice Department.* As things turned out, this was a bad message for him, for the country, and for our electoral process. Because soon Comey would again ignore clear Justice Department policy, and American history would be changed forever.

# CHAPTER SIX

# Giuliani in the Shadows?

As we will see, James Comey's October 28, 2016, letter to Congress was the final decisive act that cost Hillary Clinton the presidency. Yet it was only the visible part of an overall narrative that was deep and hidden. The complete context of that letter is important to understand: It was not an isolated event but related to an extensive network of current and retired federal law enforcement officers, centered in the New York City FBI office and apparently some in Washington headquarters as well. These retired or active officers, according to many press reports, fed negative information about Hillary Clinton and ongoing investigations to former FBI agents or reportedly to the former mayor of New York City, Rudy Giuliani. The former mayor had become well known for his political opposition to Clinton. But more than that, he was well known for his hatred of Clinton that was so personal and so venomous, fed by his outspoken support for Donald Trump, that some in the media and the political arena sometimes publicly wondered whether he appeared to be mentally unbalanced.

Here is how the final began. On September 21, 2016, Britain's *Daily Mail* broke the story that Huma Abedin's estranged husband, Anthony Weiner, was under legal suspicion for sending improper texts to an underage female. Abedin was, of course, the loyal and widely respected aide to Hillary Clinton who had worked for Clinton since her time in the White House. Weiner was the former New York City congressman who had suffered a dramatic fall from grace for sexting photos of himself to various adult women. On September 26, New York FBI agents seized Weiner's laptop. Within a couple of days, the agents found it contained about six hundred thousand of Abedin's emails, and a view of the metadata at the top of those emails, without knowing what was in the contents, indicated that some of them were to or from Hillary Clinton.

Then, as Peter Elkind of the *New Yorker* described in a lengthy report published in collaboration with the public interest investigative journalistic organization ProPublica, Comey first learned about the discovery of some of Hillary Clinton's emails on Weiner's laptop on October 3, 2016: "By this point, the email controversy had receded as an issue in the presidential race. Any news of the discovery would surely have profound consequences, especially as the election drew ever closer. Yet, over the following three weeks, FBI agents proceeded unhurriedly with their investigation, on the premise that what they knew of the discovery was not, as one official put it to me, 'investigatively significant.'"[1]

Elkind went on: "More than three weeks had passed from the time that Comey and his top deputies had been alerted to the initial discovery of Clinton emails on Weiner's laptop."

This meant that conceivably, for up to twenty-four days—from October 3 to October 27—there was no senior level decision by Comey and his top aides about what to do about the emails found on Weiner's laptop, no evidence that New York FBI agents pushed for such a meeting before then. Why the delay?

Elkind reported that on October 21, Joon Kim, the deputy U.S. attorney for the Southern District of New York, called an official in the deputy attorney general's office at Main Justice in Washington to ask what was being done about Clinton's emails on Weiner's laptop.

Joon wrote a memo noting the call. The official he talked to said this was the first they had heard about it—reinforcing the impression, well established, that Comey felt no obligation to keep his superiors at Justice informed about the Clinton emails investigation.

However, not surprisingly, such a vague inquiry would not have triggered any action by even senior officials at Justice to investigate the matter, since they—unlike James Comey—took seriously the unvarying practice, which had governed Republican and Democratic leadership at the Department of Justice for decades, to do nothing (other than actions required to save lives) in the sixty days or less prior to a presidential election.

We know with certainty that if Comey had ordered a warrant after he first heard about these emails on October 3, within a week the FBI team would have determined that there were no State Department–related emails that could justify opening another criminal investigation. We know this because, in fact, when the FBI obtained a warrant on October 30, two days after Comey sent his October 28 letter to Congress, Comey ordered an expedited review of the emails by FBI agents to try to complete the review before Election Day, eight days hence. In fact, the team that examined the Clinton emails were able to complete the search, using keywords to eliminate duplications, within seven days.

Instead, because of this inexplicable slow-walk to obtain a warrant and begin the review, it wasn't until Sunday, November 6, two days before Election Day, that Comey issued his public statement that no emails had been found that would justify any further investigation of Clinton.

Why did it take so long to bring these emails to the full attention of James Comey? Certainly we know from the public record that former mayor Giuliani and either current or former FBI agents, or both, were involved in keeping the pressure on Comey publicly, criticizing his July 5 nonprosecution recommendation regarding Clinton, and seeming to put public pressure on him to reopen the investigation. Giuliani's public comments on conservative media, especially Fox News Channel, along with the amplification of his comments and other "sources" from the FBI by the alt right—the right-wing communications complex—were reminiscent of the invisible state the alt right often alluded to as an instrument of the left. The leaks and communications from the alt right, enabled and amplified through media appearances by Giuliani, were a steady beat in October, creeping into mainstream media, often without attribution, keeping the pressure on Comey to reopen the Clinton email investigation. The fact that all this was happening during the exact same time period that the Clinton emails were first discovered on Weiner's laptop did not seem to be coincidental.

Let's first examine what we know about Giuliani, his history and relationship with Comey, and his private and publicly announced interactions with former and perhaps current New York City FBI agents who weren't bashful about admitting to reporters "off the record" that they were Bill and Hillary Clinton haters.

One can speculate that Giuliani's long-standing hostility toward Hillary Clinton began with his campaign for the New York Senate in 2000. Giuliani was expected to win before, suddenly, Clinton, who was not a New York resident, decided to test the waters to run for the Senate seat. Early polls showed Giuliani in a healthy lead over former first lady Clinton. His campaign prepared a 315-page opposition research booklet against Clinton, even including eleven pages of what was described as "Stupid Actions and Remarks."[2] But things quickly turned negative for Giuliani's candidacy, in part due to his harsh and angry demeanor, complications in his marriage that became the subject of tabloids, and Clinton's own effective upstate listening tour, which left positive impressions among normally dark red Republican voters. Clinton gained the lead in the spring of 2000.

After falling behind in the polls and increasingly subject to public ridicule for some of his bizarre personal actions, Giuliani announced he was withdrawing due to having been diagnosed with prostate cancer. After her victory, he seemed to resent her for stealing the Senate seat he had assumed would be his for the taking.

During the Republican National Convention in July 2016, Giuliani's speech showed that his animus toward Clinton had not abated over the intervening decade and a half. In one memorable moment, he took out of context a statement from Clinton's House Oversight Committee testimony on Benghazi in late 2013. She had said, with exasperation, "What difference does it make?" in response to questions by Sen. Ron Johnson (R-WI) about alleged distortions in White House "talking points" that the tragedy was in part a result of an anti-Muslim video rather than a terrorist attack. Her question was about the issue of who wrote the talking points, since she followed the question by a statement that we should all be more concerned about finding out who was responsible for the murder of those four Americans and catching them.

Here is what Giuliani said at the convention: "Anyone who can say that it makes no difference how or why people serving America are killed, should not be entrusted with the awesome responsibility to protect them and us and should not be allowed to be our commander in chief."[3] Of course, she had never suggested such a thing. But this level of distortion reinforced the impression that Giuliani's hatred of Clinton was deep. At times, beginning with the convention, many media and political pundits saw his rhetoric and personal hostility toward Hillary Clinton as sometimes unhinged, beyond the norm.

Three months later, also on display to a national TV audience, was what was described in the media as a dark and angry Giuliani seen in the background while Clinton took the microphone at the annual Al Smith Dinner on October 24, 2016, in New York City, for the benefit of Catholic Charities—a ritual for more than seventy years, with white ties and roasts and lots of laughter, attended by political celebrities, incumbent presidents, and the political challengers and members of both parties. Always in good fun and good cheer—but not for Rudy Giuliani.

When Hillary Clinton spoke, as fate would have it, the former mayor was easy to see on TV behind her in the background. His angry expression as Clinton made a few jokes about him was obvious to everyone at the dinner and those watching on TV. According to an article in the *Independent*, Giuliani "sat scowling with lopsided glasses." The next morning, a Philadelphia talk show host asked Giuliani whether his reaction to Clinton's jokes about him at the Al Smith Dinner was to want to "take out a pair of handcuffs and hold them up at that point." His response was as follows: "When I see her [Clinton], I see her in an orange jumpsuit. I'm sorry, or at least a striped one. I'd have prosecuted her a year ago and probably convicted her by now."[4]

Comey also had some personal and professional history involving adverse legal positions to President and Mrs. Clinton. Comey got his first job in 1987 as a young prosecutor from the then U.S. attorney for the Southern District of New York Rudy Giuliani. One of Comey's first assignments was to work on the criminal investigation of Marc Rich, a wealthy financier and trader whom Giuliani successfully indicted for tax evasion, among other charges. Rich was in Switzerland at the time of his indictment and he never returned to the United States to stand trial, fleeing from country to country as the U.S. authorities tried to arrest him and extradite him.

After leaving Giuliani's U.S. attorney's office in 1993, Comey worked for several years as a prosecutor in Virginia before becoming a deputy special counsel to the Senate Whitewater Committee, led by Republican senator Al D'Amato of New York. That committee became known for its partisanship in trying to show wrongdoing by President and Hillary Clinton in the Whitewater deal. Yet Comey sought the job and served for a year on the investigation. Comey has never explained publicly why he was interested in a congressional Whitewater investigation of the Clintons.

Comey became U.S. attorney for the Southern District in 2002 (nineteen years after Giuliani held that position). As the new U.S. attorney, Comey inherited the ongoing criminal investigation of Bill Clinton for his pardon of Marc Rich on the last day of his presidency, January 20, 2001. It was, to say the least, unusual for a former president to be under criminal investigation by a succeeding administration. It seemed reminiscent of a banana republic, where the incoming opposing party criminally prosecutes and attempts to jail the leadership of the prior government. The grounds for the investigation of the Clinton pardon seemed equally specious. President Clinton had explained his pardon was because of a late-night telephone call he received from the prime minister of Israel, Ehud Barak, who asked him to pardon Rich. Clinton and Barak had bonded when they came close to achieving a peace settlement during negotiations at Camp David in the summer of 2000 with the Palestinian Authority president, Yasir Arafat.[5] Prior to that call, he had decided to reject Rich's pardon application. Barak's phone call on the evening of January 19, 2001, as well as one from the revered ex–prime minister and future president of Israel, Shimon Peres, were a matter of public record. As soon as the FBI agents in New York heard about the pardon, however, they immediately instigated a criminal investigation, trying to connect campaign contributions by Marc Rich's ex-wife in 1996 to Clinton's pardon of her ex-husband (along with her contributions to the Clinton Presidential Library then under construction in Little Rock).

Many prosecutors at the time saw the case, at best, as a stretch, especially since it involved an ex-president with a public record of the calls from the Israeli leaders pleading for the pardon. However, that was not Comey's reaction. Shortly after he became U.S. attorney in 2002, a memo from the New York FBI office to the FBI director in

Washington—who just happened to be Robert Mueller—was written describing Comey as "enthusiastic" about continuing the Rich criminal investigation of President Clinton. The investigation under Comey's leadership was a continuing source of media leaks, presumably by some of the FBI agents in the New York office who were working on the investigation. That office was well known, according to many media reports, for leaks to the media on cases they had a special interest in (or angst about). The leaks included possible charges besides a quid pro quo for campaign contributions and donations to the presidential library, such as obstruction of justice, campaign finance violations, and what someone close to the case described as the "kitchen sink." Comey, as a U.S. attorney, never denounced these leaks or announced an investigation of them. The irony here is that this was the same James Comey who more than a decade later appeared to have been so concerned with leaks that even their possibility provided motivation for his sending a letter to Congress on October 28, 2016.

Comey left his position as U.S. attorney at the end of 2003 to become deputy attorney general under President George W. Bush. Two years later, the acting U.S. attorney finally closed the Clinton-Rich pardon investigation, without any announcement, despite all the leaks over the years. The case, it was said, collapsed due to the absence of any facts—but without any such public concession from the prosecutors and FBI agents who kept it going for four years. Does this pattern sound familiar?

Shortly after Comey moved to Washington to become deputy attorney general, the number two position at the Department of Justice, in March 2004, he challenged the Bush White House, specifically White House Counsel Alberto Gonzales and Chief of Staff Andrew Card, who were seeking an extension of President Bush's antiterrorist surveillance program. Comey took exception to that extension—as it turned out, from reporting in later years, on an entirely technical issue, not in principled opposition to the program. No matter.

As the story got recounted in greater detail in future months and years throughout the media, "according to Comey friends and associates" (of course, never quoting Comey directly), Comey showed up in the hospital room of U.S. Attorney General John Ashcroft to block Ashcroft's signing of the president's order to extend the surveillance program. Comey faced off, as his "friends and associates" said, on "grounds of principle" against Gonzales and Card, and convinced Ashcroft not to sign the order. Somehow, the entire story of the "courageous" James Comey "defying" the Bush White House, convincing the attorney general not to sign the order and to "uphold the rule of law," generated an invitation to appear before the Senate Judiciary Committee in May 2007.[6] Under questioning from New York Democratic senator Chuck Schumer in a public hearing covered widely by the national media, Comey divulged his role in upholding what Senator Schumer and others described as "principle" and "the rule of law."

In large part because of that incident and the high-profile recounting of it by the seemingly reluctant Comey, he gained a reputation for his integrity, a reputation he was known to be proud of and to take great pains to preserve. Again, this is worth keeping in mind as the events of 2015–2016 affecting Hillary Clinton are recounted here.

Meanwhile, Giuliani had worked closely with the New York office of the FBI in the 1980s when he was U.S. attorney and had made many close friends there, according to media reports. That continued when he served as mayor from 1993 to 2001. One especially close friend was the former head of the New York FBI office, James Kallstrom, who after his retirement became a Fox News contributor, where his anti–Hillary Clinton vitriol was frequently on display.

Bethany McLean's aforementioned article in the February 2017 issue of *Vanity Fair* was one of the most extensive, multisourced reports about the background of James Comey's October 28 letter.[7] McLean got multiple quotes, both on the record as well as those without named attribution from former prosecutors and FBI agents, showing that

Giuliani and Kallstrom were friends and had worked together to put public pressure on Comey to reverse his July 2016 decision to close the Hillary Clinton criminal investigation. She also reported, as did several other investigative reporters, that Giuliani and Kallstrom worked closely with current and former FBI agents (though Giuliani subsequently denied the former) to criticize not only Comey's nonprosecution recommendation but also the failure of prosecutors in the New York Southern District office as well as at Justice in Washington to authorize an investigation of the Clinton Foundation.

McLean wrote,

> The disquiet within the F.B.I. [over Comey's July 5 nonprosecution recommendation] was made public largely by James Kallstrom, head of the F.B.I.'s New York office from 1995 to 1997. He is close to former U.S. attorney (and former New York City mayor) Rudy Giuliani, about whom he says, "When I was a young agent, he was a young prosecutor. We've known each other for 40 years . . ." In the weeks following Comey's July [nonprosecution of Clinton] announcement, both Kallstrom and Giuliani were all over conservative news outlets talking about the "revolution," as Giuliani called it, among the F.B.I. rank and file, who viewed the failure to indict [Hillary Clinton] as "almost a slap in the face to the F.B.I.'s integrity." By late September, Kallstrom was telling the *Daily Beast* that he had talked to hundreds of people, "including a lot of retired agents and a few on the job" who were "basically disgusted" and felt they had been "stabbed in the back."

McLean quoted one former prosecutor who knew Kallstrom, who said: "He is full of shit." Another said, "The fact that a retired agent [Kallstrom] is on [Fox] TV talking about a case usually proves that he doesn't know the first damn thing about it."

Ronald Hosko, who was assistant director of the FBI's Criminal Investigative Division until he retired in 2014, seemed to be criticizing the over-ideological, pro-Trump bias of Kallstrom and other anti-Clinton agents in the New York office when he said, "Some who criticize are completely unable to divorce themselves from their political beliefs, along with their feelings about the person [Clinton]."[8]

On November 4, 2016, four days before the election, the *Guardian* published a detailed report reinforcing the widely held understanding that the FBI's New York office contained a cell of rabid pro-Trump and anti-Clinton agents. The headline of the article was: "'The FBI Is Trumpland': Anti-Clinton Atmosphere Spurred Leaking, Sources Say." The opening sentence summarizes this anti-Clinton complex within the Bureau: "Deep antipathy to Hillary Clinton exists within the FBI, multiple bureau sources have told the *Guardian*, spurring a rapid series of leaks damaging to her campaign just days before the election." It quoted a "currently serving FBI agent" as calling the FBI "Trumpland," then added, Clinton is "the antichrist personified to a large swath of FBI personnel" and "the reason why they're leaking is they're pro-Trump."

Another source of anger toward the Clintons from this group of FBI agents, according to the McLean report, beyond the emails and even the Marc Rich pardon, was their own inability to persuade their superiors in Washington to authorize a criminal investigation of the Clinton Foundation. The agents, of course, attributed their failure to pro-Clinton politics at "Main" Justice. But the real reason was that the New York agents couldn't produce a single fact to support a causal relationship between a donation to the Clinton Foundation and a favor or financial benefit in which Secretary Clinton played any role—the bare minimum needed to begin an investigation of what is, in effect, a bribery scheme. It was reported that certain New York FBI agents, especially those who were Fox News viewers, grew even angrier after the publication of *Clinton Cash*, by right-wing author Peter Schweizer, a known anti-Clinton ideologue who is also editor at large for Breitbart News. Schweizer's book cites numerous examples of donors to the

Clinton Foundation who, he tries to show, received a financial benefit from the State Department during Secretary Clinton's tenure, attempting to infer a cause-and-effect relationship between the contribution to the Foundation and the benefit from the Department, i.e., a bribe. His argument, as it turns out, confuses the distinction between correlation and causation, as in the famous example of a logical fallacy: "The rooster crows, the sun rises, therefore, the rooster causes the sun to rise."* During a Fox interview, host of *Fox News Sunday* Chris Wallace asked him to cite a single instance of such a causal relationship between a donor and a favorable State Department decision influenced by Hillary Clinton. He could not name a single one. Nevertheless, the FBI agents, in arguing they should begin a criminal investigation, in effect also confused correlation with causation.

An extensive study completed by Harvard and MIT in September 2017 on the mainstream media's bias against Hillary Clinton[9] used as a case study a *New York Times* front-page article in April 2015, mirroring similar treatment in the Schweizer book, concerning the government-approved sale of a uranium mine to Russian interests that benefited a Clinton Foundation donor. The *Times'* front-page headline read: "Cash Flowed to Clinton Foundation Amid Russian Uranium Deal."[10] The Harvard-MIT authors wrote in their report:

> Buried in the tenth paragraph of the story was this admission: "Whether the donations played any role in the approval of the uranium deal is unknown. But the episode underscores the special ethical challenges presented by the Clinton Foundation, headed by a former president who relied heavily on foreign cash to accumulate $250 million in assets even as his wife helped steer American

---

* Schweizer also told Wallace, apparently trying to show he was even-handed, that he was working on a book about former Republican governor Jeb Bush. Subsequently Schweizer published a fifty-five-page work about Jeb Bush and his business practices.

foreign policy as secretary of state, presiding over decisions with the potential to benefit the foundation's donors." Needless to say, it was the clear insinuation of corruption in the headline, not the buried admission that no evidence of corruption was in fact uncovered, that made the April 2015 story one of the *Times'* most tweeted stories during the summer [of 2016].

Moreover, the study stated the *Times* was almost certainly wrong that "whether the donations played any role in the approval of the uranium deal was unknown." The sale was approved by a multidepartment federal body called the Committee on Foreign Investment in the United States (CFIUS), including the Departments of State, Defense, Treasury, Homeland Security, Justice, and Commerce, and national security representatives, which unanimously approved the sale, as well as the independent U.S. Nuclear Regulatory Commission. Even the conservative Republican Utah Nuclear Regulatory Commission approved of this sale to Russia. It is implausible, to say the least, that all these departments and entities would have been influenced by donations to the Clinton Foundation. This was just one of many all-innuendo articles by the mainstream media that created an aura of corruption around Hillary Clinton regarding the Clinton Foundation—just part of the many excuses used by Donald Trump to back up his "Crooked Hillary" label, as he led his rally audiences in shouts of "Lock her up" during the campaign.

Yet as Bethany McLean reported in *Vanity Fair*, it appeared that New York FBI agents would not give up pressing for a criminal investigation of the Clinton Foundation, knowing full well that such an investigation would be immediately leaked and add to the bad news/innuendo/suspicion about Hillary Clinton's honesty that had already raised voter doubts because of the emails investigation.

The appearance and reality of leaks from the New York office were a major reason for Comey's decision to send the October 28 letter to Congress rather than waiting to obtain a warrant to read the emails first from Weiner's laptop, which Comey and his associates believed would be leaked.

As McLean reported: "'There is a renegade quality to the New York F.B.I.,' says a former prosecutor, which, he claims, can take the form of agents leaking to the press to advance their own interests or to influence an investigation. 'New York leaks like a sieve,' concurs another former prosecutor."

The irony, of course, is that in the name of law and order and the prosecution of Bill and Hillary Clinton, these FBI agents were willing to risk committing a felony—which is what an agent does when he or she "leaks" to a reporter the contents of an ongoing or prior criminal investigation.

When testifying before the Senate Intelligence Committee on May 3, 2017, Comey didn't exactly tell the full story when he described the timeline of his knowledge about the Clinton emails on Weiner's laptop. These are the words he used: "When the Anthony Weiner thing landed on me on October 27 and there was a huge—this is what people forget—new step to be taken, we may be finding the golden missing emails* that would change this case. If I were not to speak about that, it would be a disastrous, catastrophic concealment."[11]

It has already been noted that the emails on Weiner's laptop were discovered by New York's FBI agents investigating him on October 3.

---

* This is a fantasy that some of the most rabid anti-Clinton FBI agents carried throughout the investigation—that in the first eight weeks that Clinton served as secretary of state, she had written emails that had never been found. She was using her old BlackBerry, and the hope was that this missing trove of emails presumably contained a "smoking gun" proving her criminal intent to hide classified emails on her private server. Yet Comey's reference to this possibility as "huge" and as involving "golden missing emails" shows he bought into the fantasy and was motivated to send his letter to Congress in part because he worried it might be true and he would be blamed for "concealing" this smoking gun. Of course, we now know these "golden missing emails" did not exist.

Thus it raises the question what Comey meant that it wasn't until October 27 that the "Anthony Weiner thing landed on me." It was not until late on October 27 that Comey met with senior FBI officials and decided to send a letter to Congress about the finding of Clinton emails, even though Comey had no information at all regarding what the emails were about or whether any of them had not already been seen prior to his July 5 nonprosecution decision.

We still don't know whether Comey and his colleagues in DC intentionally slow-walked the decision to obtain a warrant and do a review of the emails before notifying Congress. But what we do know with certainty is that the New York City FBI agents knew about the Clinton emails on Weiner's laptop, even though they had not been read because the agents lacked a warrant. What also is not in dispute is that many of the New York FBI agents were openly hostile to Hillary Clinton and wanted her to lose the election. So for at least three weeks, these agents took their own sweet time before bringing this crucial, potentially history-changing information to Washington headquarters.

Why?

The *New Yorker*'s Peter Elkind asked a similar question of FBI officials in Washington: "Why hadn't agents, who had access to [Huma] Abedin's emails and could, presumably, see that she had forwarded two classified messages to her husband, taken the opportunity to examine his laptop much earlier, as part of the original email inquiry? If they had done so, what ensued in October might never have happened. The FBI declined to comment." Had they not waited so long, they would have had plenty of time to obtain a warrant, review the emails, determine there was nothing to justify a new investigation, and thus no reason to send a letter to Congress.

On April 22, 2017, the *New York Times* reported that Comey and the leadership of the FBI had assumed that the email review would take many weeks or months. Michael B. Steinbach, the former senior national security official at the FBI who worked closely with Comey, told the *Times*, "If we thought we could be done in a week, we wouldn't say anything."[12]

According to Peter Elkind, "Given the number of Clinton-related messages on Weiner's laptop (the FBI had identified 49,000 as 'potentially relevant') [far fewer than the original estimate of six hundred thousand leaked by the New York investigators and widely published in the media], no one felt confident promising the FBI director that they could be examined in time. 'I was thinking, I hope we can get this done in a couple of months,' Steinbach told me."

In the next chapter, we will return to this bogus framing of just two choices by Comey, as reflected by Steinbach and other advisers. The choice wasn't between sending a letter to Congress on October 28 and doing nothing.

Later Elkind reported that when they made the attempt, they discovered it was relatively easy to pare down the thousands of emails and complete the review in a matter of days.

The government obtained its search warrant on Sunday, Oct. 30, two days after Comey's letter, and agents immediately began scouring a copy of Weiner's hard drive, which an agent had carried to Washington from New York. . . . FBI agents had told their bosses that reviewing the new emails would take them well past Election Day. But, as the 10-member team began working around the clock, the process quickly accelerated. The FBI agents rapidly ruled out huge batches of messages that weren't work-related, 'de-duped' thousands of emails they'd seen before, and isolated the relative few—about 6,000, according to Comey [other estimates were about 3,000]—that required individual scrutiny. Potentially classified emails went to analysts for review.[13]

So here is the one clear conclusion: Had Comey been promptly informed and then promptly sought a warrant, there would have been sufficient time to review all Clinton's emails on Weiner's laptop and conclude in October—rather than two days before the election—that there was nothing new to justify opening a new investigation. The crucial, history-changing consequence is that had Comey and the FBI moved expeditiously, there would have been no Comey letter to Congress on October 28, and thus Hillary Clinton, according to all the data detailed in Chapter Eight, would have won the presidency.

In January 2017, Michael E. Horowitz, inspector general of the U.S. Justice Department, announced an independent investigation of Comey and the FBI for their overall handling of the Clinton emails investigation. Whether Comey ever communicated with Giuliani during this critical three-week time period prior to the October 28 letter should be a crucial fact to be investigated by Justice Department IG Horowitz as part of his investigation. Also, Horowitz should ask other agents in the New York office whether they ever talked to Giuliani or Kallstrom during this period or to former agents who could play the role as cutouts to leak to Giuliani, to allow him to go on Fox or other right-wing media to build pressure on Comey.

Let's look at the public statements made by Giuliani on TV (mostly on *Fox & Friends*) and radio in the three days before Comey's letter to Congress, which certainly leaves a strong inference that he was the recipient of leaked information.*

October 25: Giuliani tells *Fox & Friends*, in the context of a lengthy discussion about the FBI investigation into Clinton's email server, that "surprises" should be expected in the closing days of the campaign from the Trump campaign and perhaps from others. When the host,

---

* The information in the following time line is based on Seth Abramson, "Was Rudy Giuliani at the Center of an FBI-Trump Conspiracy to Steal the Election?" *Huffington Post*, December 21 and 22, 2016. (His answer, based on circumstantial facts and various Giuliani statements, is yes.)

Brian Kilmeade, asks if Trump has anything planned in the fourteen days before the election, Giuliani says yes—and then laughs, "ha, ha, ha," in a way that can only be described as strange, almost maniacal. "You'll see. . . . We've got a couple of surprises left." Later in the interview, he seems to imply he is referring to the FBI's Clinton investigation. Giuliani just smiled when someone on the Fox panel mentioned the FBI as the possible source of the October surprise.

October 26: Unprompted, as Fox News guest host Martha MacCallum is trying to end her interview of him, Giuliani says of Trump: "He's got a surprise or two that you're going to hear about in the next few days. I'm talking about some pretty *big* surprises."

October 28: Before the Comey letter has been publicly released, Giuliani goes on the Lars Larson radio program and says that he was the recipient of leaked information from current FBI agents, information which, with the events of the day, clearly appears to be about the Weiner/Clinton emails investigation. As CNN reported, "The former mayor said he was in contact with former agents 'and a few active agents, who obviously don't want to identify themselves.'"

That same morning, Giuliani was on *Fox & Friends*, appearing to confirm he had inside knowledge concerning the allegedly reopened emails investigation, from leaks within the FBI or from "former" FBI agents. "To tell you the truth I thought it was going to be three or four weeks ago." Then he walks back his earlier statements implying he was told about what was coming not by current FBI agents. "I heard about it from the former FBI agents," he says now. So Giuliani seems to admit that he first heard about the discovery of the Clinton emails on Weiner's computer "four weeks ago"—just a few days after September 26, when the first Clinton emails were discovered.

November 4: On *Fox & Friends*, Giuliani is asked about prior knowledge of Comey's letter to Congress and the "reopening" of the Clinton emails investigation. This time he is less discreet, although he is more careful to refer to "former" FBI agents rather than "active" ones: "Did I hear about it? You're darn right I heard about it, and I can't even repeat the language that I heard from the former FBI agents."

That same day, on CNN, Giuliani continues to walk back his original story, perhaps after realizing he has put active FBI agents and even himself at legal risk. He tries to persuade *Situation Room* host Wolf Blitzer that he didn't really mean it when he explicitly told Lars Larson on October 28 that he received information from "active" (current) FBI agents. He now claims he had "no heads-up" on Comey's letter, despite all evidence and logic to the contrary. He explains he was really referring to foreknowledge about a Trump ad campaign, although he doesn't say that the campaign ad he had in mind was about Comey's new Clinton emails investigation. (Indeed, there was no evidence that any such ad was ever created.) He also claims (not under oath, of course) that he hasn't talked to any current FBI agents in ten months.[14]

A November 4 story by Sophia Tesfaye on Salon.com summarized it all succinctly with this headline: "Rudy Giuliani Is Now Openly Boasting That the Trump Campaign Got Advance Notice of James Comey's Letter," with the sub-headline, "The Trump campaign isn't even bothering to hide its ties to the FBI at this point."

Several Democratic members of Congress called for an investigation of these leaks. Congressmen Elijah E. Cummings (D-MD) and John Conyers (D-MI) wrote: "These unauthorized and inaccurate leaks from within the FBI, particularly so close to a presidential election, are unprecedented."[15]

In the middle of all of Giuliani's TV comments came further evidence that certain elements of the FBI were involved in an effort to harm Hillary Clinton's candidacy in the closing days of the campaign.

On November 1, just one week before Election Day and four days after the release of Comey's letter, someone in the FBI Washington office released 129 pages from the Marc Rich investigation of fifteen years earlier. Why release those records so soon before the presidential election in which Bill Clinton's wife was the Democratic Party nominee? The FBI claimed it was a "routine" response to FOIA requests.[16]

*Politico*'s Josh Gerstein reported that there was no particular reason for the release under FOIA—"There was no immediate indication of any lawsuits seeking the newly posted material or that a judge had set a deadline for its disclosure." The Clinton campaign suspected political motives by the FBI for the release, which was publicized by an FBI Twitter account in a new "FBI Records Vault" that, according to *Politico*, "was dormant for about a year before suddenly springing to life on Oct. 30"—two days after Comey sent his letter. "Absent a FOIA litigation deadline, this is odd," Clinton press secretary Brian Fallon stated on Twitter, as reported by *Politico*'s Gerstein. "Will FBI be posting docs on Trump's housing discrimination in '70s?"[17]

An article on Vox.com reported that an internal investigation was triggered at the FBI to question the timing of this decision to post the Marc Rich pardon documents one week before the election. Vox's Yochi Dreazen reported on November 6, 2016:

> It's come to this: The FBI, America's premier law enforcement agency, just had to decide whether to investigate one of its own Twitter accounts to see if it had an anti–Hillary Clinton bias.
>
> The account in question, @FBIRecordsVault, burst into the news earlier this week after abruptly posting records relating to Bill Clinton's last-minute—and deeply controversial—pardon of financier Marc Rich. An FBI official said in an interview that the bureau's Office of Professional Responsibility referred the matter to its Inspection Division for possible investigation.

Moreover, Vox went on to report that "earlier this week [the week before the November 8 election], unnamed sources within the bureau told the *Wall Street Journal* that some FBI agents believed they had enough evidence to begin an aggressive investigation into a potential pay-to-play scheme at the Clinton Foundation, but were overruled by more senior officials."[18]

The timing of this FBI disclosure just before the election is suspect and should be within the scope of the Justice Department IG's investigation of Comey and the handling of the Clinton emails issue.

What does all of this mean? The answer is clear: Based on Giuliani's open prediction of surprises before the election, there does seem to have been a subterranean, anti-Clinton network at work, perhaps beginning in early 2015 and going all the way up to October 28, an active group sometimes operating independently, but with some overall common plan to do anything and everything to stop Hillary Clinton from what seemed to be her inevitable victory over Donald Trump.

CHAPTER SEVEN

# The Fallacy of the False Choice

This is the letter Comey wrote to Congress on October 28, 2016:

[To Chairs of Senate Intelligence, Judiciary, Appropriations, and Homeland Security and Governmental Affairs Committees; and to comparable House committee chairs]*

Dear Messrs. Chairmen:

In previous congressional testimony, I referred to the fact that the Federal Bureau of Investigation (FBI) had completed its investigation of former Secretary Clinton's personal email server. Due to recent developments, I am writing to supplement my previous testimony.

In connection with an unrelated case, the FBI has learned of the existence of emails that appear to be pertinent to the investigation. I am writing to inform you that the investigative team briefed me on this yesterday, and I agreed that the FBI should take appropriate investigative steps designed to allow investigators to review these

---

* The letter was copied to the ranking Democrats of each committee—a total of sixteen members of Congress. Comey actually suggested during his May 3, 2017, hearing before the Senate Judiciary Committee that he was surprised it leaked. That seems hard to comprehend.

emails to determine whether they contain classified information, as well as to assess their importance to our investigation.

Although the FBI cannot yet assess whether or not this material may be significant, and I cannot predict how long it will take us to complete this additional work, I believe it is important to update your Committees about our efforts in light of my previous testimony.

Sincerely yours,

James B. Comey

Director

Consider three phrases in the letter.

First: "*In connection with an unrelated case, the FBI has learned of the existence of emails that appear to be pertinent to the investigation.*"

"Appear to be pertinent"? "Appear" is used only because the writer has no clue what is true or not. He simply *doesn't know.* If Comey had some evidence that the FBI investigators had found emails that suggested new information, he could have written, "Based on what agents observed, we have reason to believe there may be new information."

Then: "*. . . to determine whether they contain classified information, as well as to assess their importance to our investigation.*" Again, Comey didn't know whether the trove of emails contained classified information or were important to the investigation.

Last: "*Although the FBI cannot yet assess whether or not this material may be significant . . .*" For the third time, Comey is telling the world that the FBI has no basis at all to assess the material. In other words, there might be nothing there.

Both Barack Obama and former attorney general Eric Holder have described James Comey as a good man. But as Holder wrote in an op-ed shortly after October 28, 2016, good men can make bad decisions.

Bad decisions is an understatement. Reckless judgment driven by an overwhelming preoccupation with self to the exclusion of all other factors—including following the rules that everyone else had to follow—is more accurate.

First, Comey was so obsessed with his self-image of being apolitical that he became vulnerable to committing an egregious political act—causing the defeat of a presidential candidate.

On the evening of October 28, after the letter had been sent and had already leaked, Comey wrote a memo to FBI agents explaining what he had done and why. He felt "an obligation" to reveal possible new email evidence concerning Clinton to Congress because, he said, "I testified repeatedly in recent months that our investigation was completed." He also was concerned about "misleading" the American people if he did not inform Congress.

Jeffrey Toobin posted a brief essay in the *New Yorker* the next day, October 29, which drew attention to the irony and inconsistency in Comey's statement. To avoid creating a misleading impression, Toobin wrote, "that's precisely what he did. . . . He had to know that his vague letter to Congress virtually demanded elaboration from 'senior government officials,' who would apply their own gloss, in the form of leaks. The responsibility for the confusion sown by these leaks, if not for the leaks themselves, belongs only to Comey. If the outcome of the Presidential election turns on Comey's action, that's his burden, and the nation's too."

The second driver of this reckless misjudgment was the rationalization that he had no choice. His only two choices, he said, were to "reveal" or to "conceal," exhibiting the fallacy of the false choice. Associates of his briefed the media that Comey believed he was between a "rock and a hard place." Given his commitment to preserving his own integrity and independence as well as the FBI's, he decided there truly was only one choice he could make—to "reveal."

He reasoned that there was no way he could read any Hillary Clinton emails without obtaining a warrant. And, as mentioned previously, he knew that the New York City FBI office had many agents who hated Clinton and thought she and her husband were corrupt. So Comey had good reason to believe that if he didn't "reveal" his next steps to Congress, there would be leaks to the media about his obtaining a warrant to look at Clinton's emails on Weiner's computer. And then members of Congress would not only go public with the new activity but also would accuse him of breaking his word and concealing the activity for "political reasons."

However, if Comey and his senior advisers were concerned about leaks if they sought a warrant, then why didn't they ask Abedin's and Weiner's attorneys voluntarily to allow the emails to be reviewed without a warrant? As has been reported in the media, both attorneys would have agreed.

Even if he never thought of asking for voluntary disclosure, he could have immediately obtained a warrant and searched the computer to determine whether there was information that Congress should be made aware of. And if there were leaks, he would deal with them by refusing to confirm—and by reminding the public that until there were any new facts—and there weren't—the FBI had nothing to say. The negative impact of such leaks on Clinton's campaign, with push-backs by the campaign that they were politically motivated, would have been far less than the impact of Comey's letter to Congress.

Moreover, Comey and his associates, in an extensive postelection spin operation to justify Comey's October 28 letter, falsely stated that he had promised Congress, and thus had an "obligation," to report if there was anything new regarding the Clinton emails. Put aside the fact that the FBI is a part of the Justice Department and that he, as FBI director, had no right to make any such commitments because investigatory agencies are not authorized to make policy (much less worry about politics). However, Comey and his senior aides misstated what he had actually promised Congress only a month earlier. When he appeared before the House Judiciary Committee on September 28, Republican Texas congressman Lamar Smith asked him whether there was a possibility that the FBI might reopen the Clinton investigation if it found "new information." Comey responded, "It's hard for me to answer in the abstract. We would certainly look at any new and substantial information."

So the operative words were "certainly look at . . ."—*not* an obligation to report anything new. And this is precisely what he could have done and should have done—"look at" the Weiner-Clinton emails first before putting anything in writing. Period.

Had he done that, he would not have written a letter, because within a week, the FBI would have been able to search Weiner's computer and determine that there were no Clinton emails that had not been reviewed earlier.

Another factor leading Comey to write the letter, according to the *New York Times* on April 22, 2017, was an email that the FBI discovered in a batch of hacked documents from an unknown source, allegedly a "Democratic operative." The email suggested that Clinton need not worry about Comey's investigation because the attorney general, Loretta Lynch, could be controlled and would not allow a prosecution of Clinton to occur. According to the article, Comey and his advisers were worried that if this email were leaked and damning new emails were found on Weiner's computer, they would face even further criticism from congressional Republicans. Then, on May 24, the *Washington Post* broke the story that this same email was, in fact, created by Russian intelligence as part of their misinformation *kompromat* techniques. Comey and associates subsequently claimed they "already knew" the email was fake and a product of Russian intelligence but nevertheless were worried that if leaked it would be misused by Republicans.[1] I don't know which is worse—that the FBI and Comey believed the fake memo was real or that they knew the Russians were involved but still were concerned about the email being misused by Republicans.


It also should have been obvious to Comey that he had no choice but to abide by Justice Department policies and not do anything eleven days before a presidential election. And he should never have even considered violating these policies because of his worry about congressional reactions after the election. If the worst case happened and Congress discovered new prejudicial emails after the election, Comey had a solid response: We followed the department policies, as we are required to do, and in any event, we had nothing factual to report prior to the election.

Let's dwell a moment on the Justice Department's long-standing policy not to take any actions (even, as one former deputy attorney general told me, an indictment for a serious crime) if an election is pending and to do so might affect the outcome. Only if there is a need to arrest and take someone off the streets who represents a danger to others, for example, is there to be an exception. Indeed, a memo is circulated in every presidential election year by the attorney general to remind Justice of these rules.

For this reason, the criticism of Comey in the legal community came from experts and former attorneys general from both parties. Two George W. Bush attorneys general, Alberto Gonzales and Michael Mukasey, criticized Comey for his decision. Two former deputy attorneys general—Larry Thompson under Bush and Jamie Gorelick under Bill Clinton—wrote a joint op-ed for the *Washington Post* on October 29, 2016, which reminded everyone about the sixty-day embargo policy that Comey had knowingly violated:

Decades ago, the department decided that in the 60-day period before an election, the balance should be struck against even returning indictments involving individuals running for office, as well as against the disclosure of any investigative steps. The reasoning was that, however important it might be for Justice to do its job, and however important it might be for the public to know what Justice knows, because such allegations could not be adjudicated [meaning a final verdict after due process of law], such actions or disclosures risked undermining the political process. A memorandum reflecting this choice has been issued every four years by multiple attorneys general for a very long time, including in 2016. . . .

When they take their vows and assume office, senior officials in the Justice Department and the FBI become part of these traditions, with an obligation to preserve, protect and defend them. . . . They owe a solemn obligation to maintain that credibility. They [read: Comey] are not to arrogate to themselves the choices made by the Justice Department and honored over the years.

A group of nearly one hundred former federal prosecutors and senior Justice Department officials, including former Obama attorney general Eric Holder, issued an open letter on October 30, making the same case concerning Comey's letter:

. . . Setting aside whether Director Comey's original statements in July were warranted, by failing to responsibly supplement the public record with any substantive, explanatory information, his letter begs the question that further commentary was necessary. For example, the letter provides no details regarding the content, source or recipient of the material; whether the newly discovered evidence contains any classified or confidential information; whether the information duplicates material previously reviewed by the FBI; or even [quoting from Comey's letter] "whether or not [the] material may be significant."

These former prosecutors and senior Justice Department officials added, "The fact remains that the Director's disclosure has invited considerable, uninformed public speculation about the significance of newly discovered material just days before a national election."

Republican and Democratic pundits and editorial boards also criticized the Comey decision, from right to left and in between. The conservative columnist George Will wrote, "This is a content-less October surprise . . ." He called Comey's letter to Congress "baffling," adding, "The duty of the FBI is to investigate, and when it thinks it has concluded an investigation, to pass its conclusion on to the prosecutorial arm of the Department of Justice, not to write letters to the legislative branch of government." And the *Washington Post* editorialized that the timing of Comey's letter was "unfortunate, given its potential to affect a Democratic process in which millions of people are already voting" and "set[s] a precedent that future partisans who are unhappy with the results of the FBI investigations may exploit."

The Justice Department is a huge governmental organ with some 113,000 employees. The people at its top are political appointees who have reached their positions by dint of hard work, intelligence, and outstanding records. This is also to say that James Comey had bosses at the department. There has been much oblique reporting that Attorney General Lynch and Deputy Attorney General Yates were opposed to his sending the October 28 letter before he sent it. But I have talked to multiple sources about what really happened on the dramatic day, October 27, when the AG and DAG learned that Comey was seriously considering sending his letter.

The discussions were carried on indirectly, using intermediaries. Representatives of both the attorney general and the deputy attorney general and the FBI director carried their arguments back and forth. The reasons for the underlying policy against doing or saying anything that might influence an election were stressed as being meant to avoid any appearance of political interference. Ironically, the arguments back from the director's representatives were similar—avoid even the appearance of being involved in political considerations. Each side recognized the validity of the other's arguments, but both knew they were not the principals.

Throughout the day, it was apparent to the FBI representatives that if the attorney general or the deputy attorney general felt that strongly, either should pick up the phone or visit Comey and order him not to send the letter. Of course, they were concerned that Comey might go public with the order and, whether he did or did not, that the order would leak to members of Congress, and the attorney general and/or deputy attorney general would be hauled up before congressional committees, accused of obstruction of justice, and perhaps be the subject of an FBI criminal investigation. That was implied by some of those representing the FBI director, but never explicitly. But it certainly worried those representing the Office of the Attorney General. Leaks again! Everyone was worried about leaks . . . and politics . . . and political and legal consequences.

The ultimate irony is that I have heard from both sides that had it even once occurred to Attorney General Lynch or Deputy Attorney General Yates or James Comey that the writing of a vague letter to Congress *would cause Donald Trump to win the election*, everyone would have acted differently. Lynch and Yates would have ordered Comey not to send the letter, and if he made a public fuss or there were leaks, "to hell with it," as one person close to Yates told me. The *New York Times* wrote a comprehensive narrative about these discussions in April 2017, and one of Comey's top advisers, Michael Steinbach, is on the record saying as much, that they didn't think the letter would have the effect of electing Trump.

Even President Barack Obama reportedly would have acted differently had he imagined that withholding the information he had about Russian hacking intentionally aimed at helping Trump be elected president would enable Trump to win the election. It has been reported that Comey wanted to write about the dangers of Russia's interference in the election in an op-ed but was talked out of it by the Obama White House for fear that Trump would add force to his political argument that the election was "rigged" against him. In a postelection analysis, the *Washington Post* quoted White House advisers to Obama expressing regret for his decision not to go public with the facts about Russian meddling in the election on behalf of Trump. Had Obama actually thought there was any chance of Trump winning the election, insiders have suggested, he would never have made such a decision. "I feel like we sort of choked," said someone from the Obama White House.[2]

So each player in this drama made his or her own calculations to be risk averse—the attorney general and deputy attorney general not to order Comey not to send the letter; Comey to send the letter; and Obama not to publicize what he knew about the pro-Trump Russian hacking and meddling in the election—all because they didn't think Trump had a chance. By being so risk averse, they took the greatest risk of all, at least to those who believe Trump's election was a setback for America.

Meanwhile, Comey ordered his FBI team to work around-the-clock reviewing all of Huma Abedin's emails to determine whether there was anything in them that might affect his earlier judgment that Clinton had not committed a prosecutable offense. They found the task of going through six hundred thousand-odd emails less daunting than they had anticipated and less time-consuming as well. They did a simple keyword search to narrow the number down to fifty thousand emails that had Hillary Clinton's name or State Department email addresses and her name associated. From those, they narrowed down a final search to around three thousand that conceivably might have contained classified information and might not have been reviewed before. Within several days, they determined definitively that only about a dozen or so had arguably classified information, but none of those were marked classified; and more important, *all* had been previously seen and digested when the nonprosecution recommendation was made and announced on July 5.

As reported by the *New York Times*, in the wee hours of the morning on Saturday, November 6, 2016, the agents in New York had reached a conclusion: *Nothing new here.* Comey was informed about 6 A.M. Several hours later, he wrote his letter and released it to the public to announce the nonresults:

November 6, 2016
Dear Messrs. Chairmen:

I write to supplement my October 28, 2016 letter that notified you the FBI would be taking additional investigative steps with respect to former Secretary of State Clinton's use of a personal email server. Since my letter, the FBI investigative team has been working around the clock to process and review a large volume of emails from a device obtained in connection with an unrelated criminal investigation. During that process, we reviewed all of the communications that were to or from Hillary Clinton while she was Secretary of State.

Based on our review, we have not changed our conclusions that we expressed in July with respect to Secretary Clinton.

I am very grateful to the professionals at the FBI for doing an extraordinary amount of high-quality work in a short period of time.

Sincerely yours,
James B. Comey
Director

Comey would now experience his ultimate nightmare. He could have said as much by simply writing:

Dear all:

Oops. We never should have written the October 28 letter. Sorry.

Sincerely,

James Comey

And then he could have gone to the forest and watched a tree falling with only him there noticing. Because his letter was too little, too late.

Indeed, the chairman of the Clinton campaign, John Podesta, stated that Comey's November 6 letter hurt Clinton because it put the word "emails" back into the news for the last two days before Election Day.

In any event, the Trump campaign and most Republicans on the stump for Trump ignored the letter entirely, with Trump leading the cheers "Lock her up" as if the FBI had never recommended no prosecution and as if the October 28 letter had not turned out to be about nothing. "Lock her up" was the emblem of the Trump campaign's utter disregard for the truth or facts, and unfortunately, the audiences that chanted down to the last night before Election Day seemed convinced that he was right and that the FBI was part of the "rigged" system that Trump had claimed as the reason he might lose.

We now know that Trump and most of his campaign expected him to lose. But there were stirrings somewhere that the collapsing numbers of Hillary Clinton voters, especially in the key states of Pennsylvania, Michigan, and Wisconsin, might . . . just might . . . lead to a miracle for Trump when all the votes were in.

So now we turn to the hard data. And the data is clear. But for Comey's October 28 letter, Hillary Clinton would have been elected president, and by a substantial margin.

# CHAPTER EIGHT

# Comey's Letter Elects Donald Trump

There are four ways to measure the negative effects on Clinton's standing during the time period from immediately after the letter was published through Election Day: (1) media coverage—quantitatively and qualitatively; (2) substantial increases in negative "feelings" or sentiments toward Clinton; (3) abrupt declines in national popular vote polls; and (4) even more severe declines in polls of the key battleground states.

All four of these effects of the Comey letter are proven by multiple sources of data. The evidence and the data show, conclusively, that but for the Comey letter, Hillary Clinton wins the presidency.

### 1. The Comey letter triggered overwhelmingly negative and dominant media stories about Clinton in the closing days of the election.

Most Americans still at least hazily remember the shock wave of media that broke soon after the arrival of the Comey letter in the offices of twenty-four members of Congress a little before 1 P.M. on October 28. Within minutes—surprise!—news of the letter was posted in a tweet, and mischaracterized, by the highly partisan anti-Clinton Republican chair of the House Oversight Committee, Utah's Jason Chaffetz. His tweet said, inaccurately: "case reopened."

The media went into hysteria mode. BREAKING NEWS scrolled across every cable news screen. Front pages of news websites and the next day's newspapers screamed out warnings about a "new" Clinton emails investigation, some using the word "criminal."

Probably—and predictably—the worst and most inaccurate, irresponsible headline and article came from FoxNews.com: "Hillary Clinton's Criminal Investigation: A 'Constitutional Crisis' Like Watergate."

That headline came from comments made by a former pollster of President Jimmy Carter, Pat Caddell. Also in the story was a comment from a veteran Democratic pollster, Doug Schoen, who cohosted an online Fox program with Caddell and said that he was reconsidering his support of Clinton because if she were elected, there would be a constitutional crisis.

Nate Silver wrote on FiveThirtyEight about the media coverage immediately after the letter was leaked: "The story exploded onto the scene; Fox News was treating Chaffetz's tweet as 'breaking news' within 15 minutes, and the FBI story dominated headlines everywhere within roughly an hour."[1]

The number of Google hits on all the negative words that consistently depressed Hillary Clinton's poll numbers throughout the campaign—"emails," "investigation," "FBI"—shot up. For example, just the terms "Clinton FBI" and "Clinton email" increased fiftyfold and almost tenfold respectively within a day.

Silver continued,

Few news organizations gave the story more velocity than *The New York Times*. On the morning of Oct. 29, Comey stories stretched across the print edition's front page, accompanied by a photo showing Clinton and her aide Huma Abedin, Weiner's estranged wife. Although some of these articles contained detailed reporting, the headlines focused on speculation about the implications for the horse race—"NEW EMAILS JOLT CLINTON CAMPAIGN IN RACE'S LAST DAYS."

The *Times* gave the story such major coverage, Silver points out, even though it strongly suggested that Clinton would still win. Of course, the letter was a big story and deserved front-page treatment. But the reason for this level of coverage, despite the letter's tentative and speculative contents? Silver theorized that the *Times* covered the letter as it did because it saw Clinton as the almost certain next president—and Trump as a historical footnote. By treating the letter as a huge deal, it could get a head start on covering the next administration and its imbroglios. It could also "prove" to its critics that it could provide tough coverage of Democrats, thereby countering accusations of liberal bias (a long-standing hang-up at the paper). So what if it wasn't clear from the letter whether Clinton had done anything wrong? The *Times* could use the same weasel-worded language it often does in such situations, speaking of Comey's letter as having "cast a cloud" over Clinton.

In a sense, the paper of record may have made a version of the same mistake that Comey reportedly did. The newspaper's editors and reporters needed to consider how their own actions might influence the outcome and invalidate their assessment. That influence was substantial in Comey's case and marginal for the *Times*, as one of many media outlets covering the story. But the media's choices as a whole mattered, and the tone of campaign coverage shifted substantially just as voters were going to the polls.

In fact, Clinton's voter support started to sag immediately. FiveThirty-Eight and several other polling organizations that compile all the respectable national and state polls found that her support immediately dropped 3–4 percent nationally, and more in most battleground states. The intensely negative, often inaccurate and distorted, virtually round-the-clock media coverage of Clinton in the closing eleven days of the campaign and continuing throughout Election Day without a doubt cost her heavily among voters, especially, the data shows, among "late deciders" and working-class, rural voters in key states.

The dominant and overwhelming negative media treatment of Clinton immediately after the Comey letter was extensively documented by the Shorenstein Center at Harvard's Kennedy School. The center tallied, read, and evaluated the substance of all the stories written after the letter and found abrupt and stark negative shifts against Clinton during the last eleven days of the campaign when so many undecided and swing voters were making up their minds.

For example, the quantity of media stories referring to Clinton's emails, "investigation," and the word "scandal" went from fourteen on October 23 to thirty-seven by Election Day. The print, broadcast, and cable news organizations selected by Shorenstein to study tallied one hundred stories, forty-six of which were on the front page, about or mentioning emails and referring to Comey's letter. The *New York Times*, for example, blanketed its front pages with stories about the letter, beginning on October 28, when seven stories on the letter disclosing no new facts were on the front page, with a color photograph of Clinton and her senior aide Huma Abedin.

The qualitative analysis—evaluating the "tone" of a story, whether clearly negative or clearly positive—by the Shorenstein researchers also found a major negative shift against Clinton. Measuring the ratio of negative "tone" versus positive "tone," Shorenstein researchers found that Clinton went from October 23, less than a week before the Comey letter, with a rating of -2 or -3, to -50 by October 30—a drop of *48 points* in a week's time. In contrast, the opposite happened to Trump. The tone of his media coverage shifted, relatively speaking, more positively from October 23 to 30: from -81 to -38 by Election Day—a positive increase of 43 (or, more accurately, a reduction in negative).

That represents an astonishing, cataclysmic net shift against Hillary Clinton. There was no event that occurred to cause this level of a negative shift other than Comey's letter.

The data news aggregation website Memeorandum performed a similar quantitative and qualitative analysis of news coverage post–Comey letter and showed the same results as Shorenstein. This one was broken down day-by-day, morning and evening, from October 20 to November 7, the day before Election Day. The Memeorandum website developed a mathematical algorithm that tracked which stories were gaining the most traction in the mainstream media. Comey's letter was the lead story on six out of seven mornings from October 29 to November 4, pausing for only a half day when *Mother Jones* and *Slate* published stories alleging ties between the Trump campaign and Russia. Here are the daily results:

| | MORNING (9 A.M.) | EVENING (5 P.M.) |
|---|---|---|
| Oct. 20 | Debate recap | Will Trump accept election results? |
| 21 | Trump campaign palace intrigue | Multiple systems attack |
| 22 | Trump hotels to drop Trump name | Trump sexual assault accusations |
| 23 | Trump sexual assault accusations | Polls |
| 24 | Terry McAuliffe investigation | WikiLeaks/Podesta |
| 25 | Breitbart coordination with Democrats | Trump campaign palace intrigue |
| 26 | Newt Gingrich vs. Megyn Kelly | Trump's Hollywood star vandalized |

Source: FiveThirtyEight

|  | MORNING (9 A.M.) | EVENING (5 P.M.) |
|---|---|---|
| 27 | Trump campaign palace intrigue | Trump campaign palace intrigue |
| 28 | Oregon/Ammon Bundy standoff | **Comey letter/Clinton emails** |
| 29 | **Comey letter/Clinton emails** | **Comey letter/Clinton emails** |
| 30 | **Comey letter/Clinton emails** | **Comey letter/Clinton emails** |
| 31 | **Comey letter/Clinton emails** | **Comey letter/Clinton emails** |
| Nov. 1 | Trump/Russia ties | Polls |
| 2 | **Comey letter/Clinton emails** | **Comey letter/Clinton emails** |
| 3 | **Comey letter/Clinton emails** | **Comey letter/Clinton emails** |
| 4 | **Comey letter/Clinton emails** | Terror threat |
| 5 | *National Enquirer* and Trump | Early voting data |
| 6 | Trump Secret Service scare | Trump campaign palace intrigue |
| 7 | Polls [showing Clinton declining] | Polls |

Source: FiveThirtyEight

## 2. Voter "sentiments" or feelings toward Clinton shifted negatively by a substantial margin in the days following the Comey letter.

Another study—this one perhaps the most meaningful in terms of demonstrating voter movement against Clinton and toward Trump—was performed by a consumer survey/marketing company called Engagement Labs. This organization conducts systematic surveys of consumers online to measure "sentiment," "feelings," etc., for a candidate, not black-and-white polling on who they say they are going to vote for. Engagement Labs describes their survey as conducting "conversations" with voters to determine their "sentiments"—in this case, Clinton versus Trump, beginning in mid-September and continuing through the weekend before Election Day.

Brad Fay, chief commercial officer of Engagement Labs, reported the results in a March 6, 2017, article posted on the *Huffington Post*.[2] They were, to use Fay's word, stunning. Most political scientists and observers believe that the key salient factor determining a voter's choice for president is this non-issue-based, personal "sentiment" or "feeling" toward the candidate as the voter approaches Election Day, especially among "soft" or undecided voters at the end of a campaign.

Prior to the Comey letter, Fay reported, both Clinton and Trump had net negative sentiments toward them, with Trump's exceeding Clinton's. However, after Comey wrote and published his letter, the huge change against Clinton measured by voter sentiments was impossible to deny. See the graph below:

CLINTON AND TRUMP NET SENTIMENT

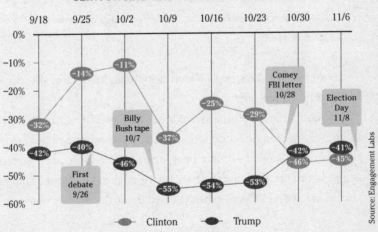

Note that the graph depicts Clinton's substantial increase in net negative sentiments, from 29 percent to 42 percent, almost entirely in the two days immediately after the Comey letter hit the media, from

October 28 to 30. Similarly, Trump's relative improvement from -53 percent to -42 percent is also shown to be in the same two days. That is a total net increase in negative voter feelings toward Clinton versus Trump of *24 points in two days*.

Fay's analysis from the Engagement Labs survey also showed that the Comey letter had an effect of accelerating the "Republicans come home" trend and may have discouraged Democrats and depressed turnout. Fay wrote:

> The Comey letter . . . did make a difference . . . in the motivation of Democrats to vote. The drop in net sentiment for Clinton was largest for Democrats at -19 points, while it remained unchanged for Republicans. Meantime, in the week of the Comey letter release, Trump's net sentiment improved by 21 points among Republicans and by 6 points among Democrats. Thus it appears that the experience of these conversations depressed Democratic turnout at the last minute while increasing it for Republicans, *making Trump's narrow victories in states like Wisconsin, Michigan, and Pennsylvania possible* [emphasis added].

As everyone knows, had Clinton won these three states she would have won the presidency.

Fay concluded, "Humans are a herding species, susceptible to sudden changes in direction when confronted with the right stimuli, and when surrounded by other people of like-mind who are impacted by the same stimuli. Comey's letter provided the stimuli for a sudden change in the peer influence dynamic that drove the election outcome."

A more traditional method of measuring voter's feelings toward a candidate is the question whether the voter has a "favorable" versus "unfavorable" opinion of the candidate. As noted in previous chapters, Clinton's "favorable impression" ratings had been net positive in healthy double-digit margins during her tenure as secretary of state. Then when the email story was first reported in March 2015 and the criminal investigation was concluded in July, Clinton's ratings turned negative through the rest of the campaign, often by double-digit margins. But by mid-October 2015 there was a definite movement reducing her net negatives down to single digits and heading to 50-50 or even positive by Election Day. This could be seen in three separate independent national polls, all conducted in the same time period between October 20 and 24 (i.e., ending four days before the Comey letter). In the Reuters/Ipsos poll of 1,506 voters, Clinton's negative impressions exceeded her favorable ones by 6 percent—53 percent unfavorable versus 47 percent favorable. Similarly, in the AP-GfK national Internet/website poll of 1,546 adults taken during the same four-day period, the same results were reported—Clinton had a net -6 rating (44 percent favorable, 50 percent unfavorable). And in the Suffolk University/*USA Today* poll taken during the same period, consistently ranked as one of the most reliable, Clinton's net minus unfavorable impression was down to 1 percent.

So while there was some apparent tightening of the race in the week before the October 28 letter, by a point or two toward Trump as "Republicans came home," there is no doubt that Clinton was trending upward as voters were giving her increasing favorable ratings and decreasing unfavorable ratings, while Trump remained as he always was during the campaign, substantially net negative in voters' opinions of him. It was the expectation of most pollsters that Clinton would continue to gain as the calendar approached Election Day, November 8.

And then came the first poll results reflecting the Comey letter (conducted from October 26 to 30). The well-respected ABC News/

*Washington Post* national poll of 1,776 registered voters reported Clinton at net -21 percent. In other words, as compared to the three previous polls completed before the Comey letter, Clinton's net unfavorables had increased by 16–22 percent in a couple of days.

From that point on through Election Day, every major national poll showed double-digit net-negative unfavorable ratings for Hillary Clinton. Gallup reported a net negative for the last week's polling of 17 percent favorable versus unfavorable opinions of Clinton. There could be no doubt that Comey's letter had caused this substantial negative shift—put simply, the bottom fell out.

## 3. Post-Comey letter, Clinton's national popular vote polls immediately declined by a significant margin.

In national polling, a shift of one or two points in a short period of time is significant; more than that is unusual—and not likely to occur unless some substantial negative event has occurred affecting one candidate and has been taken up big-time by the national media.

That is why, as we shall see, the almost immediate drop in Hillary Clinton's margin over Trump of about 4 percent within a couple of days, found in several major independent polls, was virtually without precedent. No other reason, no other event, could explain it, in that short time period of a couple of days after October 28—other than the impact of the Comey letter.

As Nate Silver of FiveThirtyEight concluded in his definitive analysis of media coverage: "The sharpness of [Clinton's] decline—with Clinton losing 3 points [nationally] in a week—is consistent with a news-driven shift, rather than a gradual reversion to the mean."

Silver tracked the effects of the Comey letter from October 28 through Election Day. Clinton's lead had declined by 3.8 percent by Election Day.

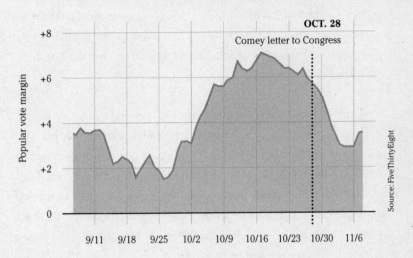

CLINTON'S LEAD CRATERED AFTER THE COMEY LETTER

Clinton's vote margin, FiveThirtyEight polls-only forecast

Silver's popular vote projection as of 12:01 A.M. on October 28 showed Clinton up 5.9 percent. For those who have criticized all of Clinton's mistakes as the reasons for her loss, or her lack of message, or her failure to "connect" with working-class voters, this margin of 6 percent as of October 28 is substantial—greater than Obama's margin over Mitt Romney in 2012 and almost as large as Obama's margin in 2008 after the economic meltdown and the collapse of Republican John McCain's candidacy. But, Silver wrote,

> a week later—after polls had time to fully reflect the Comey letter—
> Clinton's national popular vote lead had declined to 2.9 points. That
> is to say, there was a shift of about 3 percentage points against
> Clinton nationally shortly after the Comey letter. And it was an
> especially pernicious shift for Clinton because (at least according
> to the FiveThirtyEight model) Clinton was underperforming in

swing states as compared to the country overall. In the average swing state, Clinton's lead declined from 4.5 percentage points at the start of October 28 to just 1.7 percentage points on November 4, a drop of 2.8 points in less than a week—more than three times the margin that she lost in Pennsylvania and Wisconsin (.7 percent) and more than 14 times the margin that she lost in Michigan (.2 percent).

In other words, if Clinton was up +5.9 percent as of October 28 nationally among all states, then by definition she must have been up by a lesser amount in the battleground states (4.5 percent, according to Silver, which follows, since she was up by substantial double digits in California, New York, and in general the northeast and west coast states). Thus, the impact of Comey's letter was especially critical for Clinton because her margin was tighter in the battleground states, where the election would be won or lost.

Nate Silver disputed critics of Clinton's campaign by pointing out that despite all her mistakes, the race was "not even close" as of October 28. He wrote: "The standard way to dismiss the [Comey] letter's impact is to say that Clinton never should have let the race get that close to begin with. But the race *wasn't* that close before the Comey letter; Clinton had led by about 6 percentage points and was poised to win with a map like on page 150, including states such as North Carolina and Arizona (but not Ohio or Iowa). My guess is that the same pundits who pilloried Clinton's campaign after the Comey letter would have considered it an impressive showing and spoken highly of her tactics."

Sam Wang, of the Princeton Election Consortium, also independently reported that his aggregate of polls showed the same lead as Silver by Clinton over Trump of +6 percent as of October 28, 2016.*[3]

Confirming Silver's and Wang's findings through aggregation of polls were the results of the "panel study" by Dan Hopkins of the University of Pennsylvania of the same 1,075 voters, polled and repolled during the campaign. The panel also showed a 4 percent drop in numbers for Clinton during the period from the last tally of the panel (the period ending on October 24) and the voters' reporting to Hopkins after the election was over for whom they voted.

As it turns out, Hopkins could ascertain the movements of these voters in three categories, which helped explain why they dropped off Clinton's column:

- *Those who switched from Trump to Clinton or vice versa.* In the post–Comey letter period, none switched to Clinton, but Trump picked up a net gain of 1.8 percent of the vote: a 0.9 percent loss from Clinton to Trump, and +0.9 percent from third parties or undecideds to Trump. That tells us a lot: *The Comey Effect caused almost 1 percent of the voters in the panel to switch from Clinton to Trump. Note that this alone, if it had not happened in Pennsylvania, Michigan, and Wisconsin, would have changed the results of the election and Hillary Clinton would be president.*
- *Those who switched from previously undecided or third-party backers.* Trump picked up a net +0.8 percent.

* Wang wrote that he made the adjustment regarding the issue that later gave the *New York Times'* Nate Cohn concerns about the certainty of the Comey Effect, doubts he expressed in his May 8, 2017, *New York Times* piece. He pointed out Clinton's decline in some polls prior to October 28 (which was actually no more than 1–2 points in the two weeks prior to October 28, as Republicans showed signs of "coming home"). He surmised that the failure to pick up this decline in a poll the *Times* had taken in Florida, showing Trump slightly gaining, was due to the time lag between the dates the polls were conducted and the published dates of the results a couple of days later. Wang said he adjusted the data by several days to avoid "time travel," but it made no difference. The national lead by Clinton was still about 6 percent as of October 28.

- *Those who switched to third-party candidates or went undecided.* Trump picked up +1.4%.

Total Trump pickup: +4 percent.

Hopkins also notes signs that the pre–October 28 shift, if any, to Trump was a normal phenomenon of Republicans coming home, as many other analysts have reported. "Between mid-October and our post-election wave [survey], Trump picked up almost 4 percentage points from people who had backed Romney four years before, suggesting that Republican identifiers were doing just that" (and, one must assume, were encouraged to do so by all the negative media coverage of Clinton relating to the "new emails investigation").

Interestingly, Hopkins reported that the same group of people had been used as a polling panel in 2012 and that Barack Obama was ahead by 7 percent during about this same time period.*[4] In other words, the Hopkins panel represents the best single proof that Clinton was running about the same as Barack Obama performed in 2012 in her results in the 2016 election, even though the economy in the Rust Belt and working-class and rural areas had declined or stagnated since 2012. This result undermines those who tend to want to compare Clinton's political performance unfavorably to Barack Obama's in 2008 and 2012.

In sum, regarding the Comey Effect on Clinton's standing versus Donald Trump in the immediate days after he sent his letter: It is

---

* The Obama panel had 6 percent less undecided (of course, Obama did not suffer the dramatic effects of a letter). A "panel" polling approach randomly selects a statistically significant number of people and then polls and repolls them on a regular basis. This avoids possible disparities with normal polling methodology—picking a different random sample for each poll. There are pluses and minuses with each approach. In this case, both produced approximately the same result during about the same time period. Hopkins explains the purpose of an ongoing panel rather than different samples each time: "Panel surveys differ from other polls in that they re-interview the same people repeatedly, allowing us to see how specific Americans' attitudes shift over time. They thus help us sidestep the problem that some groups of people might be more likely to take polls when their candidate is thought to be doing well or receiving favorable press coverage."

telling that three polling organizations, independent of one another—FiveThirtyEight, the Princeton Election Consortium, and Dan Hopkins's University of Pennsylvania panel study—all arrived at almost exactly the same percentage measuring the adverse impact of the Comey Effect on Hillary Clinton's national popular vote—about 4 percent downward on Clinton's margin over Trump in the first week after it was sent.

Even with the effect of Comey's letter, she defeated Donald Trump with almost three million more votes than he received. Without it, say if she had maintained the margin of 6 percent she had on October 28, she would have defeated Trump by about eight million votes.

### 4. Clinton's lead plummeted by an even larger margin in the key battleground states immediately after the Comey letter—costing her a majority of electoral votes.

Here is a table using the RealClearPolitics weekly polling averages between Clinton and Trump in Pennsylvania, Michigan, and Wisconsin on October 28, before Comey's letter was publicly released; on November 7, one day before the election; and the final results on Election Day.

| POST–OCTOBER 28 SHIFT IN CLINTON SUPPORT (PERCENT) | | | | |
|---|---|---|---|---|
| As of | 10/28 | 11/7 | 11/8 | Net Clinton Drop—11 days |
| Pennsylvania | +5.0 | +0.6 | −0.7 | −5.7 |
| Michigan | +6.5 | +3.4 | −0.2 | −6.7 |
| Wisconsin | +6.5 | +6.5 | −0.7 | −7.2 |

Source: RealClearPolitics

Clinton lost Pennsylvania, Michigan, and Wisconsin by a collective total of 78,000 votes out of a total of 13.8 million votes, or about six-tenths of 1 percent. Looking at the voter drop in each state,

Clinton dropped a total of 5.7 percent, or approximately 347,000 votes, in Pennsylvania; 6.7 percent, or approximately 306,000 votes, in Michigan; and 7.2 percent, or approximately 210,000 votes, in Wisconsin in just eleven days. There was no intervening event other than the Comey letter that could have caused such a precipitous decline. Even if there were "hidden" Trump supporters, particularly in the rural, working-class areas in these three states, areas in which Trump showed greater strength than Mitt Romney had experienced in 2012, there were still not enough voters there to account for the severe drop by Clinton and gain by Trump in such a brief period of time. In short, it is hard to argue that, in the absence of the Comey letter and all the negative media about it, Hillary Clinton would not have done at least 0.8 percent better in Pennsylvania and Wisconsin and at least 0.3 percent better in Michigan and won the presidency with 278 electoral votes. And her likely gain of just 1.3 percent in Florida without the Comey letter's devastating effects would have won her that state. She would also have won North Carolina and Arizona, where polls showed her with a narrow lead over Trump as of October 28.

Silver also noted in his May 3, 2016, analysis that as of October 28, "Clinton led . . . by 6 to 7 points in polls of Michigan, Wisconsin, and Pennsylvania. Her leads in Florida and North Carolina were narrow, and she was only tied with Trump in Ohio and Iowa. But it was a pretty good overall position."

Silver then compiled two scenarios. The first one was more conservative, in which Clinton gained only 1 percent more votes in the key battleground states in the absence of the Comey letter, which he called the Little Comey Effect. In the second scenario, Silver assumed Clinton would have picked up 4 percent of the vote in the key battlegrounds if there had been no Comey letter, which he calls the Big Comey Effect.

Here is a table showing the results of both effects:

| ADJUSTED VOTE MARGIN* | | | | |
|---|---|---|---|---|
| | Clinton Vote Margin | Little Comey Effect* | Big Comey Effect* | Clinton's Electoral Votes Had She Won |
| Michigan | −0.2 | +0.8 | +3.8 | 248 |
| Pennsylvania | −0.7 | +0.3 | +3.3 | 268 |
| Wisconsin | −0.8 | +0.2 | +3.2 | 278 |
| Florida | −1.2 | −0.2 | +2.8 | 307 |
| Nebraska's 2nd C.D. | −2.1 | −1.1 | +1.9 | 308 |
| Arizona | −3.5 | −2.5 | +0.5 | 319 |
| North Carolina | −3.7 | −2.7 | +0.3 | 334 |
| Georgia | −5.1 | −4.1 | −1.1 | 350 |
| Ohio | −8.1 | −7.1 | −4.1 | 368 |
| Texas | −9.0 | −8.0 | −5.0 | 406 |
| Iowa | −9.4 | −8.4 | −5.4 | 412 |

Source: Nate Silver

Let's recall how narrow the margin was in Pennsylvania, Michigan, and Wisconsin on Election Day, relying on the January 3, 2017, *Cook Political Report*'s "certified results":

| | % Clinton | % Trump | % Difference | Vote Difference |
|---|---|---|---|---|
| Pennsylvania | 47.9 | 48.6 | 0.7 | 44,292 |
| Michigan | 47.4 | 47.6 | 0.2 | 10,704 |
| Wisconsin | 47.0 | 47.8 | 0.8 | 10,704 |
| Total difference: 77,744 votes ÷ 13.8 million = 0.6% | | | | |

* Adjusting for the Little Comey Effect adds 1 percentage point to Clinton's margin; a Big Comey Effect adds 4. Hypothetical scenario starts with the 232 electoral votes Clinton actually won, ignoring electors who changed their votes.

As the table shows, Clinton would have won the presidency if Nate Silver's very conservative assumption of a Little Comey Effect of 1 percent increase in these three states had occurred in the absence of the Comey letter. Indeed, less than that increase in the Clinton vote would have elected her president—with a gain of just 0.3 percent in Michigan and 0.8 percent in Pennsylvania and Wisconsin.

Nate Silver produced the electoral vote map below that shows what he describes as the "Big Comey Effect" depicted in the chart on page 149—i.e., with Clinton suffering a -4 percent drop in popular vote polls nationally (which, as we saw, was found by multiple independent poll aggregators and the University of Pennsylvania panel). Assuming Clinton was not harmed by this 4 percent margin because of the Comey letter, then with no Comey letter Clinton wins not only Pennsylvania, Michigan, and Wisconsin but also Florida, Nebraska's second congressional district, Arizona, and North Carolina—for a total of 336 electoral votes:

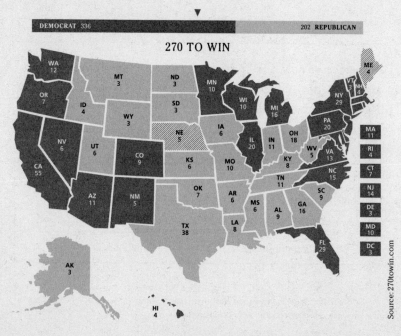

Probably the most compelling case for the negative power of Comey's letter over Clinton's candidacy is the table displayed in a Vox study.[5] Policy/elections experts Sean McElwee, Matt McDermott, and Will Jordan averaged all the RealClearPolitics polls in the battleground states on three dates:

- October 21, the week before the Comey letter
- October 28, the day of the letter
- November 7, the day before Election Day

| LATE SHIFT IN THE BATTLEGROUND STATES (Trump lead in RealClearPolitics) | | | | | |
|---|---|---|---|---|---|
| | 10/21 | 10/28 | 11/7 | Result | Polls post-10/28* |
| Virginia | −8 | −8 | −5 | −5.3 | 6 |
| Colorado | −7.2 | −5 | −2.9 | −4.9 | 7 |
| Maine | −5.2 | −5.2 | −4.5 | −2.7 | 1 |
| Nevada | −4.2 | −1.6 | 0.8 | −2.4 | 4 |
| New Hampshire | −8 | −5.2 | −0.6 | −0.4 | 7 |
| Michigan | −11.6 | −6.2 | −3.4 | 0.2 | 5 |
| Wisconsin | −7 | −6.5 | −6.5 | 0.7 | 2 |
| Pennsylvania | −6.2 | −5 | −1.9 | 0.7 | 6 |
| Florida | −4 | −0.7 | 0.2 | 1.2 | 6 |
| Arizona | −1.3 | −1.5 | 4 | 3.5 | 1 |
| North Carolina | −2.5 | −2.4 | 1 | 3.7 | 4 |
| Georgia | 4 | 2.8 | 4.8 | 5.2 | 5 |
| Ohio | 0.6 | 1.5 | 3.5 | 8.1 | 3 |
| Iowa | 3.7 | 1.4 | 3 | 9.4 | 3 |
| AVERAGE | −4.1 | −3.0 | −0.5 | 1.2 | |
| *individual pollsters counted only once | | | | | |

Source: McElwee, McDermott, and Jordan

The result of these comparisons is breathtaking proof of the devastating, game-changing impact of Comey's letter on Hillary Clinton's presidential candidacy.

The table shows that as of October 28, Clinton would have won the battleground states of Virginia, Colorado, Maine, New Hampshire, Michigan, Pennsylvania, Florida, Arizona, and North Carolina, which, combined with the states she won on November 8, gives her 333 electoral votes to Donald Trump's 205, a tally almost identical to the FiveThirtyEight Big Comey Effect scenario depicted on page 149, which showed Clinton with 336 electoral votes.

And since her trend lines would likely have gone up without all the saturated negative media driven by the Comey letter after October 28, she was close enough possibly to pick up Georgia, where she was behind by fewer than 3 points; Ohio, behind by 1.5 percent; and Iowa, with a deficit of 1.4 percent.

Also in the Vox article, the policy/election experts compared the results of absentee ballots cast prior to the October 28 letter with actual Election Day results. This was a rough way to measure the impact of the letter, like the late deciders who were polled by exit day pollsters. If there was a substantial disparity between the results of absentee ballots, which were presumably close to a cross section of all voters in the state (assuming both campaigns had relatively equivalent absentee ballot efforts, which they did), and actual results, then that disparity would be strong evidence of the Comey Effect.

## Rhode Island

The Vox article shows this disparity in this deep blue state, strongly Democratic and for Hillary Clinton. A serious gap/falloff here from the absentee ballot split to the final results would provide strong evidence of the adverse Comey Effect. In 2012, President Barack Obama received 61 percent of the absentee ballots in Rhode Island,

and in 2016 Clinton received 60 percent. On Election Day, Obama did about the same (slightly better, by 5 percent).

But in the eleven days between the pre–Comey letter total and Election Day, Clinton's support in the state dropped 13 points. That is huge—and inexplicable except for the impact of Comey's letter.

## Florida

The same substantial Clinton drop-off occurred in Florida. This critical state was in a virtual dead heat, according to the last RealClearPolitics average, prior to October 28. Clinton won the absentee ballots 52 percent to 48 percent (excluding the Libertarian and Green Party votes), but the comparable two-party spread on Election Day was +12 percent—56 percent Trump and 44 percent Clinton. That type of swing cannot be explained entirely by increased turnout in the rural and working-class Trump areas.

## Steve Schale/Central Florida/the Critical I-4 Corridor

The Vox writers reported on the results of Steve Schale, the well-known Florida political consultant and strategist who had managed Obama's successful 2008 campaign and who had predicted, based on early voting before Comey's letter, that Clinton would carry Florida.

Schale examined the crucial swing-vote area around the I-4 corridor, in the central portion of the state, including Orlando and Tampa Bay and Daytona Beach. He found that Clinton won the early vote with 56.3 percent of the two-party vote compared to only 47.3 percent on Election Day. Vox reports that this was a "highly unusual gap suggesting a pretty significant surge."

\* \* \*

The data on late-deciding voters may be some of the strongest evidence demonstrating the impact of the Comey letter. Since nothing significant happened in the last week other than the letter, the huge disparity in the results of these late deciders compared to the total state results must have been caused or heavily influenced by Comey's letter. There is some counterpoint to this argument, that voters who wait till the last week to make up their minds often lean against the incumbent or, in the case of Hillary Clinton, the "establishment" candidate. On the other hand, given Donald Trump's enormous personal negatives on character, temperament, behavior, qualifications, and fitness for office in all the polls, it may be more likely that these late deciders who didn't like Hillary Clinton were still ready to vote for her, even "holding their nose," given how fearful they were of Trump.

The most reliable way to assess these late deciders is through exit polls. Pollsters are stationed outside polling places throughout a state, gathering a random sample of thousands of voters (and thus low margins of errors), asking them not only whom they voted for but also why.

Here is the revealing, and maybe the most compelling, data about voters in the key battleground states who waited until the last week before deciding whom to vote for—again, compiled in the Vox article.

| VOTERS WHO DECIDED THEIR VOTES THE WEEK BEFORE THE ELECTION (EXIT POLL DATA) (PERCENT) | | | | |
|---|---|---|---|---|
| | Clinton | Trump | Margin of difference | Trump margin |
| Wisconsin | 30 | 59 | Trump 29 | +0.7 |
| Pennsylvania | 37 | 54 | Trump 17 | +0.7 |
| Michigan | 39 | 50 | Trump 11 | +0.3 |
| North Carolina | 41 | 59 | Trump 18 | +3.7 |
| Florida | 38 | 55 | Trump 17 | +1.2 |

Source: FiveThirtyEight

Not withstanding the narrow margins in these five states, of course, there are pundits who prefer to focus on Clinton's mistakes, which she has acknowledged, and get angry that she "blamed" Comey. Kevin Drum, a writer for *Mother Jones*, addressed those who wanted to focus on Clinton's mistakes—and it is hard to rebut his thesis that the math on October 28, 2016, speaks for itself:

> For the sake of argument, let's assume that Hillary Clinton was an epically bad, unpopular candidate who ran a terrible campaign.... If this is true, it was true for the entire year. Maybe longer. And yet, despite this epic horribleness, Clinton held a solid, steady lead over Trump the entire time.... The public still preferred her by a steady 3–7 percentage points over Trump the entire year....
>
> Basically, Hillary Clinton was doing fine until October 28. Then the Comey letter cost her 2–4 percent of the popular vote. Without Comey she would have won comfortably—possibly by a landslide—even though the fundamentals predicted a close race....
>
> If you disagree that Comey was decisive, you need to account for two things. First, if the problem was something intrinsic to Clinton or her campaign, why was she so far ahead of Trump for the entire race? Second, if Comey wasn't at fault, what plausibly accounts for Clinton's huge and sudden change in fortune starting precisely on October 28?
>
> One way or another, it appears that all the things that were under Hillary Clinton's control were handled fairly well. They produced a steady lead throughout the campaign [through October 27, 2016]. The Comey letter exists on an entirely different plane. It was an unprecedented breach of protocol from the FBI; it was completely out of Clinton's control; and it had a tremendous impact. *That's* why I blame James Comey for Donald Trump's victory.[6]

# It's Time for an Impeachment and Twenty-Fifth Amendment Investigation

The President, Vice President and all civil Officers of the United States, shall be removed from Office on Impeachment for, and Conviction of, Treason, Bribery, or other high Crimes and Misdemeanors.

—Constitution of the United States,
Article II, Section 4

As stated in the introduction to this book, the importance of demonstrating that James Comey's October 28, 2016, letter cost Hillary Clinton the presidency is not about defending her campaign or even compiling broader historical truth. As instructive as these points are, they are in the past, and now the future looms—with three more years of Donald Trump as president. And yet we know that Trump was elected illegitimately—that is, not as a reflection of the popular will expressed in an uncorrupted, fair, and free election. We know that with certainty. We know that from data that cannot be disputed. We know that but for the intervention of FBI director James Comey on October 28, sending a fact-free, entirely speculative letter to the U.S. Congress, triggering an avalanche of negative media about Clinton under a new (criminal) investigation, causing her poll numbers to drop precipitously both nationally and in the key battleground states, Clinton would have won the election with a majority of electoral votes. We know with certainty that she would have at least won the three states of Pennsylvania, Michigan, and Wisconsin but for the Comey letter, since she lost those three states by less than 1 percent each, and by a total of 78,000 votes combined in all three.

Thus we know that Donald Trump's election was a quirk, an anomaly, a fluke of James Comey's poor judgment and preoccupation with self. Whatever other reasons there may be to oppose an impeachment process investigation regarding Donald Trump, one of them *cannot* be that to do so would be to flout the popular will by overturning the electoral vote count that he would not have earned without the fluke of James Comey's last-minute improper intervention.

Add to that the irrefutable, unanimous conclusion that the Russian government and intelligence service meddled in the U.S. election in favor of Trump and harming Hillary Clinton. We may not know whether that meddling was decisive, but it doesn't matter. We know that it happened—even while Trump lies and denies it. And that further delegitimizes his election as president.

It is therefore mandatory, in light of the actions and conduct of Donald Trump in his first year as president, that an impeachment investigation process be initiated and, one would hope, on a bipartisan basis.

Special Counsel Robert Mueller is already at work investigating collusion between the Trump camp and Russia, a concept so inimical to all our country that to simply utter the notion is profoundly disturbing. Yet although indicting a president is theoretically possible, it has never happened and is not the best way to get to the truth of what the president knew and when he knew it. Moreover, Mueller is vulnerable to being fired by Trump.

There is a better way to find out what Trump has—or has not—done, which is for Congress to begin an impeachment investigation. The nation, its history, and the democratic traditions of our great republic demand no less. Our Constitution gives Congress, specifically the House of Representatives, the awesome power to get to the truth about a president's abuse of power and betrayal of the trust placed in him. And the House and Senate impeachment process is the best way to determine whether—and, if so, how—alien and hostile forces of the Russian government at the highest levels succeeded in corrupting our democracy. If there is evidence of collusion by any American, much less the president himself, then we must know that. And if there is none, we must know that too.

So now let's look at the facts that are not in dispute—and those that are unknown and need to be investigated and can best be obtained by involving the president himself through the power of the House of Representatives to conduct an impartial impeachment inquiry.

The framers sought to create a government by the people, in contrast to England's government by the privileged monarchy. Critical to this concept of self-government, they believed, was the ability to remove certain officials from office if necessary. Hence, this was one of the first provisions brought up at the Constitutional Convention in May 1787.

Despite the importance of this provision, the record of the convention contains little guidance on what constitutes grounds for impeachment. The words "treason" and "bribery" are well understood, but what constitutes "high crimes" or "misdemeanors" remains the subject of debate, particularly in the years during and after the impeachment inquiries involving Presidents Nixon and Clinton. It is important to note that the delegates' understanding of "misdemeanor" had to do with conduct of public officials and not with crimes punishable by lower sentences, which is how the word is currently used in American law.

James Madison, frequently called the Father of the Constitution, stated during the convention that a removal provision was necessary for "defending the Community ag[ain]st the incapacity, negligence or perfidy of the chief Magistrate. The limitation of the period of his service [is] not a sufficient surety. He might lose his capacity after his appointment. He might pervert his administration into a scheme of peculation or oppression. He might betray his trust to foreign powers. [His] loss of capacity or corruption . . . might be fatal to the Republic."[1]

The ratification discussions that were published as the Federalist Papers focused more on the impeachment process itself. However, these arguments often included descriptions of conduct that could lead to impeachment. Alexander Hamilton, in Federalist No. 65, wrote of the process: "The subjects of its jurisdiction are those offenses which proceed from the misconduct of public men, or, in other words, from the abuse or violation of some public trust . . . [and] relate chiefly to injuries done immediately to the society itself." Repeated incontrovertible lies by a president could be considered the abuse of a public trust.

Scholars look to American history for guidance in what conduct constitutes an impeachable offense. To date, no president has been removed from office under the impeachment clause. While several federal judges, a senator, and a cabinet secretary have been so removed, constitutional scholars point out that because a president is uniquely situated, these cases provide little understanding as to grounds for impeachment of the chief executive. However, there is general agreement that the offenses include the abuse of power that is inherent in the office of president.

Under the process set out in the Constitution, charges of impeachment are brought in the House of Representatives, and the decision to convict or acquit resides with the Senate. This was intended to prevent the process from being politicized, primarily because in 1787 senators were chosen by state legislatures and not by popular vote. This seems ironic, if not quaint, in today's hyperpartisan atmosphere. However, the constitutional requirements of a simple majority of the House to bring impeachment charges (Article I, Section 2, Clause 5) and a two-thirds majority of the Senate to convict (Article I, Section 3, Clause 6) are thought to counterbalance any political motivation.

In practice, however, there was unquestionably a partisan aspect to the presidential impeachment proceedings that have occurred to date. Rep. Gerald R. Ford stated in 1970 that an impeachable offense "is whatever a majority of the House of Representatives considers [it] to be in a given moment in history." In retrospect, what Ford, a thoughtful and moderate man, must have meant was not that it was acceptable for the House to pass a resolution of impeachment for frivolous or entirely partisan reasons (say, purely motivated as a method to overturn the presidential election results). Surely he intended that the House and the Senate were expected by the framers to decide what offenses are "impeachable" and justify the president's removal, despite the election results, based on contemporary standards and values. So Ford seems to have recognized that the framers intended the definition of an impeachable offense ultimately to be "political"—not in the partisan sense but rather the political judgment of what presidential conduct constituted "injuries done immediately to the society itself" and to the Constitution.

An analysis of the presidential impeachment proceedings to date is instructive in what conduct has led to articles of impeachment and may shed light on the possible actions by the current House of Representatives.

Three presidents have been subject to these proceedings:

- Democratic president Andrew Johnson in 1868, who succeeded Abraham Lincoln after the latter's assassination, was impeached by the House on a partisan vote but survived conviction and removal from office in the Senate by just one vote.

- Republican president Richard Nixon's impeachment was approved by the House Judiciary Committee on July 30, 1974, with bipartisan support. He resigned on August 8, before there was a vote by the full House or a trial by the Senate, after a delegation of Senate Republicans visited him the day before to urge him to resign.[2]
- Democratic president Bill Clinton was impeached by the House Republicans in a virtually entirely partisan vote. But the House initiative was rejected in the Senate. The House could not obtain a majority of the 55 Republican senators to support any of the two counts they presented for voting, much less the 67 votes required for conviction and removal.

On March 2, 1868, the House of Representatives, controlled by the Radical Republicans, passed articles of impeachment against President Andrew Johnson. This faction of the Republican Party was called Radical because its members represented the most extreme, punitive wing of the anti-Confederacy members of Congress, contrary to President Lincoln's call for the opposite approach to Reconstruction in his Second Inaugural ("with malice toward none, with charity for all").

The Radical Republicans approved eleven articles of impeachment against Johnson, a Democrat, by a vote of 126 to 47. The articles related specifically to his firing of Secretary of War Edwin Stanton in violation of the Tenure of Office Act. But the underlying conduct reflected his failure to support congressional Reconstruction efforts after the Civil War. One of the articles charged Johnson with bringing the office of the president into "contempt, ridicule, and disgrace, to the great scandal of all good citizens."[3] Only three of the eleven articles were voted on by the Senate after a trial. When none of those received the required two-thirds majority, the Senate adjourned rather than vote on the remaining eight articles.

The Senate failed to achieve the necessary two-thirds vote by only one vote—if one senator had switched from opposed to in favor, Johnson would be the only president ever to have been removed from office. Historians have found the Johnson impeachment to have been illegitimate, as it was almost entirely partisan—the opposite of what Madison, Hamilton, and the framers intended. For this reason, its illegitimacy has been described as similar to the partisan vote on President Clinton in 1999, further discussed below.[4]

One aspect of Article X among the eleven Johnson impeachment articles might be pertinent to any investigation of Donald Trump. Although most of this article can be ignored because of its patently absurd contention that it is an impeachable offense to make speeches that are disrespectful to Congress, the words of Republican congressman Benjamin Butler characterizing the content and style of these speeches might be worth noting. Butler described Johnson's speeches as "intemperate, inflammatory and scandalous harangues"—implying they were nonpresidential and brought the presidency into disrepute. Article X also referred to conduct and statements by President Johnson that were "unmindful of the high duties of his office and the dignity and proprieties thereof." In addition, it referred to statements made that were "highly censurable in any, [and] are peculiarly indecent and unbecoming in the Chief Magistrate of the United States." By his use of such intemperate and unpresidential language, Johnson was said to have brought the office of the president "into contempt, ridicule and disgrace." Some might fairly point to words and phrases used by Donald Trump as similarly unpresidential, "indecent, and unbecoming."

President Richard Nixon's articles of impeachment in 1974 included obstruction of justice, violating the constitutional rights of citizens, and failing to produce materials under subpoena. He resigned before the full House could vote on the articles. Article I—obstruction of justice—approved by the House Judiciary Committee, accused Nixon of "making false or misleading public statements for the purpose of deceiving the people of the United States" and "[acting] in a manner contrary to his trust as President and subversive of constitutional government, to the great prejudice of the cause of law and justice and to the manifest injury to the people of the United States."[5] Six Republicans crossed party lines to vote for the first article, and seven voted for Article II, and two Democrats crossed party lines to vote against the third article. One Republican, Rep. Larry Hogan of Maryland, a strong and outspoken conservative, voted against Nixon on all three articles.

In 1998, the House approved two articles of impeachment against President Bill Clinton—those relating to perjury before the grand jury (Article I) and obstruction of justice (Article II). The impeachment process regarding Clinton has been compared by many historians to the partisan and illegitimate impeachment process of Andrew Johnson, and in many respects, seen by historians as worse.[6]

Before the impeachment process began, in the November 1998 congressional elections, with the campaigns dominated by the issue of whether or not Clinton should be impeached, the Democrats actually picked up five seats over the Republicans, a result described as "stunning" by many political observers. As a result, Newt Gingrich, the rabid anti-Clinton partisan speaker favoring impeachment, resigned as speaker and announced he would leave the House by the end of the year. Moreover, the House Republican leadership pushed forward on impeachment votes on December 19, using a lame duck Congress to do so, meaning those Republicans who had been defeated in the November elections were allowed to vote. Moreover, the Republican House leadership would not even allow a roll call vote on an alternative to impeachment—a strong censure of President Clinton regarding his personal conduct. This refusal to allow a vote on an alternative to an inevitable cratering and humiliation of its impeachment resolutions was inexplicable and shameful.

Only five Democrats in the entire House supported either of the two impeachment counts, whereas 228 and 223 Republicans supported the first and second, respectively.[7]

Further supporting the partisan nature of the proceedings is the fact that the House Republicans could not obtain even a majority of 51 of the 55 Republicans in the Senate for either of their impeachment counts. Indeed, on Article I (lying to the grand jury), the House Republicans lost 55 to 45 (meaning 10 of the 55 Republican senators voted "not guilty"). On Article II, the Senate split 50–50, meaning 5 Republicans opposed the House Republicans. In contrast to Andrew Johnson, the House Republicans trying to impeach Bill Clinton fell far short of the necessary two-thirds in the Senate on February 12, 1999, by 17 and 22 votes, respectively, on the two counts.

So, what has history taught us about impeachment as a remedy to remove a president of the United States—literally, to overturn the results of the election of a president? It must meet a burden of proof so high that it can be justified only in the most extreme circumstances and it must have some signs of bipartisanship.

Susan Low Bloch of the Georgetown University Law Center has criticized the "nonchalance displayed by members of Congress, especially the House of Representatives, during the Clinton impeachment" as "wrong then and remains wrong today." She quoted the renowned Yale Law School professor Charles Black in his book on impeachment: "The election of the president (with his alternate, the vice-president) is the only political act that we perform together as a nation. . . . No matter, then, can be of higher political importance than our considering whether, in any given instance, this act of choice is to be undone, and the chosen president dismissed from office in disgrace. Everyone must shrink from this most drastic of measures. . . . [Removal is] high-risk major surgery, to be resorted to only when the rightness of diagnosis and treatment is sure."[8] In short, impeachment is a drastic measure to be contemplated only as a last resort.

Therefore, there must be a heavy presumption against even attempting an impeachment process against President Donald Trump, a sitting president. The standards for considering impeachment must be high, and the quantity and quality of factual support of any article should be even higher. The president is elected by the people, and President Trump may stand for reelection in 2020. That is the better way to remove him, if he deserves to be removed, than through the impeachment process.

However, any concern about overturning a legitimately elected president should not be applicable to Donald Trump's 2016 election. It cannot be deemed, at least using traditional definitions, as "legitimate," because of the abnormal—"alien" is not too strong a word—intervention into the electoral process by James Comey.

Another factor undermining Trump's legitimacy as president, which cannot be quantified but indisputably damaged Hillary Clinton's candidacy, is the proven intervention of the Russian government to help Trump and to harm Clinton. There is no doubt whatsoever that this happened. It is confirmed by the highest levels of the Intelligence Community, based on hard human, documentary, and other top secret intelligence sources and methods. No one disagrees with this conclusion—no one in either Intelligence Committee of either party in either chamber of Congress. It is a fact.

The president-elect was informed of this fact by Friday, January 6, 2017, with "high confidence" based on raw, highly classified intelligence, by James R. Clapper Jr., the director of national intelligence; John O. Brennan, the director of the CIA; Adm. Michael S. Rogers, the director of the National Security Agency; and James B. Comey, the director of the FBI.[9]

Yet one person in the government has refused to accept this finding—indeed, has mocked and ridiculed his own Intelligence Community in the presence of senior officials of the Russian government, including one of its top spies, during a meeting in the Oval Office:

Donald Trump. (The fact that Trump has willfully lied about and denied Russian intervention on his behalf will be further discussed below in the proposed second article of impeachment that merits investigation.)

Given that the standards for impeachment must be high, and the known facts must be sufficiently numerous and undisputed to justify even beginning an investigation, I have selected only five grounds for possible impeachment among the many possible. These are the ones with the most indisputable evidence. The overarching standard of abuse of presidential power is the common thread:

1. Obstruction of justice and cover-up, thereby threatening the rule of law and our system of justice
2. Abuse of the public trust by knowingly and willfully perpetuating lies that harm the national interest and faith in government and undermine the nation's security from foreign, hostile powers
3. Attacks on the First Amendment protections of a free press
4. Words and actions suggesting betrayal of trust to a hostile foreign power
5. Conflicts of interest constituting self-enrichment involving possible violations of the Constitution's two separate provisions prohibiting domestic and foreign emoluments

## Obstruction of Justice and Cover-Up

Whether President Trump's firing Comey as director of the FBI, asking for his personal loyalty, or asking him to back off on the investigation of his former national security adviser are criminal obstructions of justice is not relevant. The only relevant issue is whether these actions constituted impeachable offenses as understood from prior interpretations of that term as well as contemporary judgment of abuse of power and trust by the U.S. Congress. If the facts show that Trump abused his power as president to thwart the fair and effective operation of the criminal justice system of our government to protect himself and/or his colleagues, that would be an impeachable offense.*

This is how the House Judiciary Committee defined impeachable "obstruction of justice" actions of Richard Nixon in their Article I that they voted to approve on July 27, 1974:

> On June 17, 1972, and prior thereto, agents of the Committee for the Re-election of the President committed unlawful entry of the headquarters of the Democratic National Committee in Washington, District of Columbia, for the purpose of securing political intelligence. Subsequent thereto, Richard M. Nixon, using the powers of his high office, engaged personally and through his close subordinates and agents, in a course of conduct or plan designed to delay, impede, and obstruct the investigation of such illegal entry; to cover up, conceal and protect those responsible; and to conceal the existence and scope of other unlawful covert activities.

On June 8, 2017, Comey, who had been fired the month before by President Trump without notice while he was on the West Coast

---

* Obstruction of justice is knowingly and purposely interfering, by word or deed, with a federal judicial proceeding or a pending proceeding before Congress or a federal agency, or even an informal investigation by an executive agency. It is easy to understand but hard to prove.

Alan Dershowitz argues that since the president has the power to fire the FBI director and could have issued a pardon to prevent any prosecution of Michael Flynn, then doing either cannot be a criminal offense. Moreover, he argues, since President Trump has that constitutional power, examining his motives is irrelevant, even irresponsible. But with all due respect, motives may be irrelevant in a strictly constitutional separation-of-powers context but not in the context of judging impeachable offenses involving the abuse of presidential powers and the public trust. If Trump's motives included a desire to thwart the criminal justice system to protect himself and his associates from being exposed about collusion with the Russians during the campaign, then those motives would be reasons for impeachment and removal from office. See Alan Dershowitz, "Trump Did Not Obstruct Justice in Firing James Comey," *Washington Examiner*, May 11, 2017.

giving a talk to FBI employees, testified before the Senate Select Committee on Intelligence:

> The President began [the January 27 dinner at the White House] by asking me whether I wanted to stay on as FBI Director, which I found strange because he had already told me twice in earlier conversations that he hoped I would stay, and I had assured him that I intended to. He said that lots of people wanted my job and, given the abuse I had taken during the previous year, he would understand if I wanted to walk away.
>
> My instincts told me that the one-on-one setting, and the pretense that this was our first discussion about my position, meant the dinner was, at least in part, an effort to have me ask for my job and create some sort of patronage relationship. That concerned me greatly, given the FBI's traditionally independent status in the executive branch.
>
> I replied that I loved my work and intended to stay and serve out my tenure term as Director. And then, because the setup made me uneasy, I added that I was not "reliable" in the way politicians use that word, but he could always count on me to tell him the truth. I added that I was not on anybody's side politically and could not be counted on in the traditional political sense, a stance I said was in his best interest as the President.
>
> A few moments later, the President said, "I need loyalty, I expect loyalty." I didn't move, speak, or change my facial expression in any way during the awkward silence that followed. We simply looked at each other in silence. . . .
>
> Near the end of our dinner, the President returned to the subject of my job, saying he was very glad I wanted to stay, adding that he had heard great things about me from Jim Mattis, Jeff Sessions, and many others. He then said, "I need loyalty." I replied, "You will always get honesty from me." He paused and then said, "That's what I want, honest loyalty." I paused, and then said, "You will get

that from me." As I wrote in the memo I created immediately after the dinner, it is possible we understood the phrase "honest loyalty" differently, but I decided it wouldn't be productive to push it further. The term—honest loyalty—had helped end a very awkward conversation and my explanations had made clear what he should expect.*

Here is an analysis of Comey's testimony by Philip Allen Lacovara, a former U.S. deputy solicitor general in the Justice Department and counsel to Watergate special prosecutors Archibald Cox and Leon Jaworski. Lacovara concluded that Comey's testimony, if true, sets out a criminal case of obstruction of justice, regardless of whether or not the president can be indicted. (Most scholars do not believe he can be until he leaves office.) Lacovara laid out evidence "sufficient for a case of obstruction of justice."[10]

Lacovara wrote, "The president had specifically attempted to shut off at least a major piece of what Trump calls the 'Russia thing,' the investigation into the misleading statements by fired national security adviser Michael Flynn concerning his role in dealings with the Russians. This kind of presidential intervention in a pending criminal investigation has not been seen, to my knowledge, since the days of Richard Nixon and Watergate."

Lacovara went on to say, "Comey's statement meticulously detailed a series of interventions by Trump soliciting his assistance in getting the criminal probe dropped. These details are red meat for a prosecutor." Comey was "sufficiently alarmed" that he chose to write what he recalled of the conversation in various contemporaneous memoranda, including immediately typing one memo on his laptop in his car.

The director of national intelligence, Daniel Coats, and National

---

* Trump and his personal attorney challenged many of Comey's assertions in this testimony, in effect accusing him of committing perjury. But their denials were not specific or documented—exactly the reason why a congressional impeachment is needed. Only that investigation can compel testimony and documents from the president.

Security Agency director Mike Rogers were asked by President Trump to issue statements asserting that Trump was not under personal investigation. They denied that they "felt pressured." But Lacovara concluded that statement "provides no comfort for the president's position. The obstruction of justice statute prohibits not only successful interference with pending criminal investigations but also any use of 'threats' to 'endeavor' to obstruct an investigation. It is the attempt or objective that is criminal—even if it fails—and Coats and Rogers were apparently unable to deny that the president had solicited their interference in the pending FBI investigation. If Coats and Rogers did not yield to the endeavor, kudos for them, but that is no excuse for the president."

Comey also articulated the element of what he perceived as "threats" during his dinner with the president, limited to the two of them. Leaving little doubt about the price of continued retention, the president twice, according to Comey, told him that he expected "loyalty" from Comey, just as he did from everyone else around him.

On February 14, 2017—the day after Michael Flynn was forced to resign as the president's national security adviser when it was learned that he had lied to Vice President Pence and to others about his prior Russian contacts—the president "carefully structured another one-on-one meeting with Comey, specifically ordering Attorney General Jeff Sessions, to whom the FBI director ordinarily reports, to leave the Oval Office where Comey, Sessions, and other national security officials (and Jared Kushner) had been meeting." At that point, the president laid his cards on the table, according to Comey: "I hope you can see your way clear to letting this go, to letting Flynn go. He is a good guy. I hope you can let this go."*

---

* This also possibly showed that Trump was aware that he had something improper in mind when he asked to speak to Comey alone. Otherwise, why would he ask everyone else to leave the room, including and especially his attorney general, Jeff Sessions, who arguably could have insisted on staying as the appropriate thing to do?

Lacovara suggests that further evidence of pressure on Comey to protect the president rather than to do his duty as FBI director were in Trump's phone calls on March 30 and April 11, "asking Comey's help in removing the 'cloud' over Trump resulting from the FBI investigation into Russian interference in the 2016 election and possible Trump campaign collusion. The president again demanded loyalty: 'Because I have been very loyal to you, very loyal; we had that thing you know.' He pressed Comey to make public statements exonerating the president, but Comey declined to do so."

The president's firing of Comey on May 9 constituted further evidence, according to Lacovara, of obstruction of justice—as did his complicity in Vice President Mike Pence's public false statements (and those of White House spokespersons) that Comey was fired because of the recommendation of the deputy attorney general, Rod Rosenstein. Trump knew these statements were false when they were made, yet he said nothing to correct them publicly. But two days later, when it was reported that the deputy attorney general would not remain quiet in the face of this blatantly false explanation, Trump was forced to tell the truth, calling in *NBC News*'s Lester Holt. As Lacovara wrote, Trump "brazenly stated that he fired Comey in order to bring the 'Russia thing' to a close, and he [a few days later] bragged to senior Russian officials in a private Oval Office meeting that this is what he thought that he had accomplished by sacking Comey."

Lacovara summarized the case for obstruction:

Comey's statement lays out a case against the president that consists of a tidy pattern, beginning with the demand for loyalty, the threat to terminate Comey's job, the repeated requests to turn off the investigation into Flynn and the final infliction of career punishment for failing to succumb to the president's requests, all followed by the president's own concession about his motive. Any experienced prosecutor would see these facts as establishing a prima facie case of obstruction of justice.

It is also not true that "motive" is irrelevant in an obstruction case involving the president when the issue is impeachment as opposed to criminal prosecution. As Richard W. Painter and Norman L. Eisen, top White House ethics officers under Presidents George W. Bush and Barack Obama, respectively, wrote on May 17, 2017:

> What [the president] cannot do is exercise that power [to fire the FBI director] corruptly, to spare himself or those associated with him, like Mr. Flynn, from scrutiny and possible criminal liability. To do so would run afoul of a series of federal statutes that define the crime of obstruction of justice. They are variations on the theme that anyone who "corruptly" or by "any threatening letter or communication" tries "to influence, obstruct, or impede, the due administration of justice" will be subject to criminal penalties.[11]

To sum up: Regardless of whether the president can or cannot be indicted, the impeachable offense is the abuse of presidential power "corruptly" to interfere with, impede, and possibly thwart the operation of the U.S. criminal justice system. That abuse subverts the rule of law, due process, and equal protection and application of the laws under the Constitution. Thus, if these allegations are proved true, then there are reasonable grounds for impeachment and removal of President Trump from office.

Another element for investigation is the possibility that Trump obstructed justice and abused his presidential powers by attempting to intimidate a witness—Director Comey, and what was discussed during their private conversations. On May 12, three days after Trump fired Comey, the president posted a message on Twitter, which some (including Comey) regarded as a threat: "James Comey better hope that there are no 'tapes' of our conversations before he starts leaking to the press!"[12]

This statement could be reasonably regarded as an attempt to intimidate Comey—and, at the very least, requires further investigation. On June 22, Trump finally stated that he did not make any tapes and had no tapes (which is not the same as saying that no tapes exist).[13] For no apparent reason, for more than four weeks Trump refused to confirm or deny whether he had such tapes, adding to the suspicion that he was attempting to intimidate or influence Comey in future testimony. If he was bluffing with his tweet, that raises the question whether he was intentionally misleading the public.

In addition, Trump's calls to the two top intelligence agency officials from the CIA and the NSA to seek their help regarding the ongoing FBI criminal investigation inevitably evoke powerful memories of and analogies to the Nixon cover-up and forced resignation.

According to media reports, on March 22 President Trump discussed the Flynn investigation during a White House meeting with National Intelligence director Daniel Coats and CIA director Mike Pompeo. The president reportedly complained about the investigation and sought Director Coats and Director Pompeo's assistance in curtailing the FBI investigation.

Two days after that meeting, President Trump called Director Coats to request he release a statement denying any evidence of coordination between his presidential campaign and the Russian government. The president also repeatedly called the director of the National Security Agency, Mike Rogers, with the same request. When both men were asked to describe those calls when they testified in public before the Senate Intelligence Committee, they refused. (They reportedly answered questions in a private, executive session.)

Recall that it was the White House audiotape of Nixon telling his chief of staff, H. R. Haldeman, to pressure the CIA to be part of the Watergate cover-up that became the "smoking gun" that caused Nixon to resign. On August 7, 1974, a Republican congressional delegation told Nixon that he did not have the votes to avoid conviction and removal. The result was Nixon's resignation two days later.

One of the provisions of the articles of impeachment against Nixon referred to his "endeavoring to misuse the Central Intelligence Agency." Those words appear to be chillingly applicable to President Trump's calls to the CIA's Coats and the NSA's Rogers. Those calls would certainly merit further investigation if a preliminary impeachment investigation on obstruction of justice were to occur.

### Abuse of Public Trust: Serial, Willful Material Lies

Alexander Hamilton, in Federalist Paper No. 65, wrote that impeachment offenses "are those offenses which proceed from the misconduct of public men, or, in other words, from the abuse or violation of some public trust. They are of a nature which may with peculiar propriety be denominated POLITICAL, as they relate chiefly to injuries done immediately to the society itself."

A comprehensive legal memorandum written by President Bill Clinton's personal attorneys and the leaders of the Office of the White House Counsel during his impeachment process list all the possible standards constituting impeachable offenses accumulated over the years by scholars, interpreting the words, intent, and spirit of the Founders when they drafted, debated, and made the final judgment on the words to use in the impeachment clause in the Constitution.[14] The list can be fairly summarized in the Hamiltonian concept: To be guilty of an impeachable offense, the president of the United States must engage in an abuse of the powers of his office that, in the judgment of the House and Senate, constitutes an attack on the system of government and on our constitutional checks and balances, or as Professor Charles Black of Yale Law School put it succinctly, constitutes "serious assaults on the integrity of the processes of government."

In other words, the president (and vice president) of the United States are the two officials under our Constitution elected by the voters of the nation—and thus, they not only represent the entire nation but owe a duty to all voters, "to the society itself."

There is precedent in Nixon's case that a pattern of lies to cover up his abuses of power and justice is sufficient for impeachment of a president. Regarding such abuses, Lawrence Hogan, a conservative congressman from Maryland and the only Republican who voted for all three articles of impeachment in the Nixon case, in part explained his vote this way: "The evidence convinces me that my President has lied repeatedly, deceiving public officials and the American people."

For a lie to be impeachable, therefore, it must be serious enough to be termed "material"—having a substantial, adverse impact on the nation and the American people, as Hamilton stated, "injuries done immediately to the society itself." Therefore, if Trump were found to have systematically told the American people material lies, amplified by the power and prestige of his office and with immediate access to the media, this would constitute a classic abuse of power and, thus, an impeachable offense.

The *Washington Post* has calculated that since January 21, 2017, Trump's first day as president, he has told one thousand lies. Whether or not any or all of these documented falsehoods are "material" and thus possibly impeachable and justifying removal remains to be seen.[15]

Among the material lies that could be the basis for an impeachment investigation is the outright lie, which Trump could not justify but never repudiated, when he accused Barack Obama of wiretapping him and his colleagues at Trump Tower. That was an attack on a former president for committing a felony as president. This certainly meets the standard of "materiality"—a vicious statement that Trump knew was untrue when he said it, and thus was unable to offer any evidence for whatsoever. This is the type of lie that undermines the office of the president. It was as much of a bald-faced lie as Trump's multiyear lie before he became president that President Obama was not a U.S. citizen, which he refused to retract and repudiate even after Obama made public his birth certificate.

Another example of a Trump lie that could be found to be material and the basis of impeachment is his claim that the almost three million voters who constituted Hillary Clinton's margin over his number of popular votes in the presidential election were illegal, undocumented immigrants. This is a particularly insidious abuse of power because as president he is telling the nation that our electoral system is so porous and subject to fraud that our democratic processes cannot be trusted. That is literally an attack on our society, our system of government, our election officers, and the integrity of our democracy.

Perhaps the worst and most damaging lie of all is Donald Trump's denial that Vladimir Putin intervened in our presidential election and hacked, meddled, and corrupted our democratic processes to undermine our system of government—and specifically to help him and harm Hillary Clinton. That is a direct threat to our nation and to our system of government. Donald Trump's attack on our Intelligence Community by mocking and denying their findings and downplaying the significance of the Putin-directed meddling is, literally, a failure to defend our nation from a foreign hostile attack on our most important election.

Since his inauguration, Trump has repeatedly denied or falsely suggested that it is unknown or unclear or unproved that the Russians intervened or "meddled" in the 2016 election.[16] These denials continued even after the January 6 briefing by the directors of the FBI, CIA, National Security Agency, and national intelligence—the leaders of the Intelligence Community. The president-elect was given a copy of the classified report, which revealed direct raw intelligence (such as documents, observations, intercepts, etc.) proving this pro-Trump/anti-Clinton interference directed by Russian president Vladimir Putin.[17]

Trump's subsequent and repeated public denial of these facts could be found by congressional impeachment investigators to be knowing, intentional, and willful misstatement—the definition of a lie. Thus, if determined to be material and serious by a House committee, this lie alone would be an impeachable violation of the public trust and fiduciary duties every president owes to the American people.

Evidence of "materiality" might be deemed to exist in Trump's repetition of the lie just before and during the G20 summit on July 7–8, 2017, in Hamburg, Germany. He stated the lie in front of the world's media as well as the leaders of Western Europe and Russia. Two days before, on July 5, in Warsaw, Trump stated that "nobody really knows" whether any Russian hacking occurred. He lied again when he said it was "possible" (and later added "probable") that the hacking was done by other countries.[18] This was subsequently denied as lacking any evidence at all by the director of national intelligence, James Clapper.[19]

In addition, in July 2017, President Trump appeared to have put himself in the middle of a potential charge of lying to the media and the public about, and possible knowing cover-up of, his campaign's collusion with the Russian government to meddle in our presidential campaign. On June 9, 2016, Trump's son, Donald Jr., met with someone identified in an email to him as a Russian "government lawyer." The email stated that this lawyer intended to disclose "incriminating" information about Hillary Clinton possessed by the Russian government, and that the government favored Trump over Clinton. Donald Jr.'s reaction expressed in a responding email—rather than, as required, by notifying the FBI immediately that a foreign, hostile government had approached the Trump campaign to interfere in America's most important election—was: "I love it."[20]

The first question for an investigative impeachment process would be: Did Trump's son tell his father about this meeting and share the contents of the emails? After the story broke in the *New York Times* on July 10, 2017, President Trump denied knowing about the meeting. Many doubted that could possibly be true. A meeting based on what the email described as anti-Clinton incriminating information, supplied by the Russian government, seems to be the kind of information that any son active in the campaign would immediately bring to Dad.

In any event, this is precisely the kind of key factual dispute—perhaps the difference between Trump being impeached and removed from office or not—that only a congressional impeachment process would be able to try to resolve. If, for example, it could be established that Trump knew about this meeting and had read the emails, then all of his denials of the Russian meddling would be, without any doubt, lies. And, of course, a congressional committee could find an impeachable offense in colluding with Russia to corrupt our election to help himself get elected.

Perhaps almost as serious was Trump's possible involvement in creating the first false and misleading statement issued by Donald Jr. in response to the *New York Times* story about the June 9, 2016, meeting. According to the *Times*, "as Air Force One jetted back from Europe on Saturday [July 8, 2017], a small cadre of Mr. Trump's advisers huddled in a cabin helping to craft a statement for the president's eldest son, Donald Trump Jr. . . . explaining why he met last summer with a lawyer connected to the Russian government. Participants on the plane and back in the United States debated how transparent to be in the statement, according to people familiar with the discussions."

Debated "how transparent"? That is another way of saying, "Should we tell the truth?" Their decision was to mislead. Instead of stating that the meeting was intended to include a discussion of negative information about Hillary Clinton allegedly possessed by the Russian government, the statement said the meeting discussed only the issue of adoptions of children that had been halted due to U.S. sanctions against Russia. That was a lie—and the individuals who drafted the statement and Trump Jr. knew it was a lie. But then the *Times* reported that "the president signed off" on the statement, which was "so incomplete that it required day after day follow-up statements, each more revealing than the last."[21]

At that time, of course, Trump knew his campaign was under criminal investigation for possible collusion with the Russian government. If a thorough investigation resulted in a determination that Trump had participated in issuing misleading statements and lying to the public about that meeting, with the unavoidable inference of a criminal cover-up, that would certainly present a case for impeachment and removal from office.

It should be remembered that this impeachment standard is—as it should be—high. It's not just about a president lying. One could say that Franklin Delano Roosevelt lied or misled the American people about the Lend-Lease program, which allowed him to secretly aid the British by supplying arms to help in the war against Adolf Hitler and Nazi Germany without congressional authorization. Or John F. Kennedy, at least for a period of days, lied or misled the American people about what was going on behind the scenes in the Cuban missile crisis—as in, "President Kennedy has a cold and has to cancel all his appearances," told by the president's press secretary, Pierre Salinger, as a cover story for Kennedy meeting with his Exec Comm group of national security leaders to discuss how to deal with the crisis.

These are presidential lies, to be sure, but lies that are not harmful to the American people and interest—indeed, to the contrary, their purpose is to advance the nation's interest. Thus, they are not "material" to the issue of impeachment. And certainly, these lies were not motivated by a desire to protect the president from criminal investigation or culpability.

Even if a lie is intentional and self-serving, that does not make it impeachable. It must, as the precedents and historical and legal analyses prove, constitute a danger to the state and to the public and to the nation. Lying about and refusing to acknowledge the undeniable truth that Russia, led by its autocratic president, Vladimir Putin, engaged in a systematic campaign to interfere in the election of a president of the United States is a serious material lie. The evidence is substantial that this is what President Donald Trump did repeatedly after his inauguration.

## Undermining Faith in the Constitution—First Amendment Freedoms

The First Amendment to the Constitution states that "Congress shall make no law . . . abridging the freedom . . . of the press. . . ."

Thomas Jefferson considered the First Amendment's protection of the freedom of the press one of the most fundamental protections of the American democracy, and he said so repeatedly. For example, he famously wrote, "The basis of our governments being the opinion of the people, the very first object should be to keep that right; and were it left to me to decide whether we should have a government without newspapers or newspapers without a government, I should not hesitate a moment to prefer the latter. But I should mean that every man should receive those papers and be capable of reading them. . . ."[22]

And James Madison, the author of the First Amendment, emphasized that even more important is to protect unfettered freedom of the press even when—especially when—it is wrong, even "abusive": "Some degree of abuse is inseparable from the proper use of every thing, and in no instance is this more true than in that of the press. It has accordingly been decided by the practice of the States, that it is better to leave a few of its noxious branches to their luxuriant growth, than, by pruning them away, to injure the vigour of those yielding the proper fruits."[23]

So there can be no doubt that press freedoms are fundamental to our society and our system of government. Of course, that does not mean the media is not subject to criticism. A good part of the early chapters of this book criticize press coverage of the Hillary Clinton emails issue. (And it should be noted that freedom of the press includes the freedom of one part of the press to criticize others, such as in the instance of this book.) But there is a difference between criticizing the media, which is fair game and which every president of the United States has done, and calling the press the "enemy of the American people." A huge difference.

Such an expression by a president of the United States demonizes the media generally and, thus, uses the immense power of the presidency to undermine the freedom of the press that Jefferson, Madison, and so many others considered crucial to our nation. A president using his bully pulpit not only to depict the media as the "enemy" but also, as we have seen, enabling if not encouraging his supporters to take violence against reporters is against the law (in some cases a felony). Conceivably, his inflammatory depiction of the free press as the "enemy" constitutes an abuse of presidential power that should be the basis of an impeachment investigation.

If it is unfair to attribute the excesses of Trump's supporters to him, then at the very least we should acknowledge that Trump has done little to discourage such violence and denounce it. To the contrary. On July 2, 2017, Trump posted a tweet that portrayed himself, albeit in an altered WWE video clip, in a violent take-down of a wrestler with the label "CNN" on his head.

As reported by the *Washington Post*:

A day after defending his use of social media as befitting a "modern day" president, President Trump appeared to promote violence against CNN in a tweet.

Trump, who is on vacation at his Bedminster golf resort, posted on Twitter an old video clip of him performing in a WWE professional wrestling match, but with a CNN logo superimposed on the head of his opponent. In the clip, Trump is shown slamming the CNN avatar to the ground and pounding him with simulated punches and elbows to the head. Trump added the hashtags #FraudNewsCNN and #FNN, for "fraud news network."

The video clip apparently had been posted days earlier on Reddit, a popular social media message board. The president's tweet was the latest escalation in his beef with CNN over its coverage of him and his administration. . . .

In a statement tweeted out by CNN media reporter Brian Stelter, CNN called it "a sad day when the President of the United States encourages violence against reporters." The network cited Trump's "juvenile behavior far below the dignity of his office. We will keep doing our jobs. He should start doing his."[24]

In sum: It cannot be an impeachable offense for Trump to be very critical, and outspokenly so, of the media. But at the least, a full compilation of all of President Trump's words and actions suggesting not just criticism but such generalized hostility and demonization of a free press is necessary to determine whether an impeachable offense has occurred.

## Betrayal of Trust to the United States in Favor of Russia

As indicated, James Madison stated at the 1787 Constitutional Convention that an impeachable offense would occur if the president were to "betray his trust to foreign powers."

This standard means that any president who refuses to publicly repudiate a foreign power that has engaged in hostile acts against America and publicly disparages the unanimous findings of the U.S. Intelligence Community about those hostile acts would presumptively appear to be betraying the trust he owes to America and favoring a foreign power that has interfered in the democratic process of our country. If proved, this would seem to be an impeachable offense.*

Several instances of President Trump's words and conduct suggest such a betrayal of trust. One example is his failure to act after Deputy Attorney General Sally Yates twice visited the White House counsel at the end of January 2017 to warn him and, thus, to warn the president, that Michael Flynn was "compromised" with the Russians by his lies to Vice President Mike Pence and "underlying conduct" (which she would not define during her public hearings before the Senate Intelligence Committee). President Trump has never explained why, given that knowledge, he kept Flynn on as his national security adviser for another eighteen days and allowed him to be briefed on the most sensitive intelligence information that the president receives and to attend meetings involving such information.[25]

Further, Trump did not hesitate to repudiate the heads of the Intelligence Community on Russian leaders. A former senior government official and national security expert told me that he was "surprised and disappointed" to hear Trump deny that the Russians meddled and to label the report a "hoax." The official was offended when Trump criticized the Intel Community for allowing this "fake news" to leak out, and asked, "Are we living in Nazi Germany?"

For this reason it is worth exploring what President Trump did and was willing to say when he invited top Russian officials, including a reported top Russian spy in Washington, to the Oval Office on May 10, 2017. Trump's statements and conduct that day occurred during a meeting with Sergey V. Lavrov, the Russian foreign minister, and

---

* It should be noted that the legal concept of treason, as defined in the Constitution and in federal law, would not be applicable here. An act can be treasonous *only* if it is committed when the United States is at war with another nation. Therefore, if Michael Flynn or Donald Trump Jr. or, for that matter, President Donald Trump were found to have colluded with President Putin and the Russian government to interfere in the U.S. presidential election, that would not constitute "treason" under the law or the Constitution, since the United States is not at war with Russia.

Sergey I. Kislyak, Moscow's ambassador to the United States, said to be one of Russia's top spies.

A shocking aspect of that meeting, which suggests a Madisonian betrayal of trust and a pro-Russia bias, is that Trump barred the U.S. media while allowing Russian media, including photographers, to attend with no Secret Service or FBI monitoring or restrictions. Nor, apparently, were there any precautions to prevent the planting of bugs while Trump or his aides weren't watching. (American photographers were allowed for only a few minutes at the end of the meeting.)

According to the *New York Times*, "Colin H. Kahl, the former national security adviser to Vice President Joseph R. Biden Jr., took to Twitter to pose what he called a 'deadly serious' question: 'Was it a good idea to let a Russian gov photographer & all their equipment into the Oval Office?' David S. Cohen, the former deputy director of the C.I.A. during the Obama administration, responded: 'No, it was not.'"[26]

The meeting took place on May 10, the day after Trump fired James Comey because of the "Russia thing." Yet the president was willing to tell the top Russian officials that firing the FBI director, had relieved "great pressure" on him, according to a document summarizing the meeting.

President Trump also revealed highly classified and sensitive information to the Russians, including their spy, concerning ISIS, which the Russians and others inferred (correctly) was from Israel. According to Vox, "When Donald Trump revealed highly sensitive information to Russian Foreign Minister Sergei [*sic*] Lavrov in the Oval Office, he directly endangered the life of an Israeli spy living under deep cover in ISIS territory. . . . 'The real risk is not just this source,' Matt Olsen, the former director of the National Counterterrorism Center, [said,] 'but future sources of information about plots against us.'"[27]

Even though none of this is legally treasonous, for the reasons stated above, from an impeachment standard perspective many journalists and ordinary Americans may sense that something close to the concept of treason occurred, however unwittingly, by President Trump.

Remember that James Madison used the phrase "betrayal of trust to foreign powers" as a basis for impeaching a president. That must have been an important one for him. Madison described the debates in his diary every day, and it is clear that he was very reluctant to oust a president using impeachment unless there was a gross danger to the integrity of the government, similar to Alexander Hamilton's impeachment offense standard of an offense to the society itself governed by our Constitution.

Also, as explained above, the word "trust" has the inherent meaning of a trustee with a fiduciary duty—in this context, a duty first and exclusively to the American people and not to any foreign power, much less a foreign power such as Russia whose policies have been adverse, at times downright hostile, to the American people.

We know without doubt that as of the fall of 2017, Russia had engaged in what many have described as an act of war: a direct and intentional attack on our democracy and our democratic processes, specifically with the aim of corrupting the most important election in our nation—the election of a president. We know from the email received by Donald Trump Jr. that on June 9, 2016, the Russian government had offered, through someone identified in the email as its attorney, to provide critical information about Hillary Clinton to assist Donald Trump in his presidential campaign. Donald Jr. insists that he did not inform his father of this, but it nevertheless is the basis for a congressional investigation. If Trump knew about this or subsequent offers by Russia to assist him and harm Clinton and welcomed either, that would surely constitute the level of "betrayal of trust to foreign powers" that would meet Madison's standard—at the least, a threshold crossed to initiate an impeachment investigation.

## Violations of the Domestic and Foreign Emoluments Prohibitions

There are two provisions of the Constitution that might provide the basis for impeachable offenses if violated by the president.

Most people who have studied the emoluments issue are familiar with the "antiforeign" emoluments clause (Article I, Section 9, Clause 8), forbidding any U.S. government office holder to receive anything of value from a foreign power. The clause reads, in relevant part:

> No Person holding any [U.S. government] Office . . . shall, without the Consent of the Congress, accept of any present, Emolument . . . of any kind whatever, from any . . . foreign State.

Less familiar is what is known as the anti-domestic emoluments clause (Article II, Section 1, Clause 7):

> The President shall, at stated Times, receive for his Services, a Compensation, which shall neither be increased nor diminished during the Period for which he shall have been elected, and he shall not receive within that Period any other Emolument from the United States, or any of them.

An emolument is some form of advantage—a gift, or profit, or cash payment—due to one's official position. Both articles have been interpreted by some constitutional experts as barring any elected or appointed U.S. government official, including the president, from accepting additional economic benefit "of any kind whatever" while holding office. (Other experts, a minority, don't believe the foreign emoluments clause applies to the president.)

The framers may have believed that allowing such emoluments makes the recipient vulnerable to foreign bribes and corruption. And they had reason to worry. So, near the end of the Constitutional Convention, Charles Pinckney "urged the necessity of preserving foreign Ministers & other officers of the U.S. independent of external influence." That idea became the so-called foreign emoluments clause.*

In addition, at the Constitutional Convention, Alexander Hamilton warned, "Foreign powers . . . will interpose, the confusion will increase, and a dissolution of the Union will ensue." Hamilton also stated, in Federalist Paper No. 22, "One of the weak sides of republics, among their numerous advantages, is that they afford too easy an inlet to foreign corruption." The delegate Elbridge Gerry said, "Foreign powers will intermeddle in our affairs, and spare no expense to influence them. . . . Every one knows the vast sums laid out in Europe for secret services."[28]

Has President Trump received emoluments? Three lawsuits have been filed in DC federal district court since January 2017, asserting that he has violated one or both of the Constitution's emoluments provisions, foreign or domestic, by allowing himself to be economically benefited by foreign governments, such as when foreign diplomats stay in Trump hotels or he profits from foreign deals and decisions; or allowing his salary to be supplemented while serving as president through such continued ownership of U.S. hotels and assets. The first suit was filed in January by CREW, Citizens for Responsibility and Ethics in Washington, and amended in April to include local restau-

---

* Those who argue that this clause was not intended to apply to the president of the United States don't address the fact that the president is not specifically exempted, and that the exact words used do include the president: "no Person *holding any Office* [of the U.S. government] . . ." (emphasis added). Moreover, the context and thrust of the discussion at the convention, as can be seen from Pinckney's remarks, were concern about "external influence." Only the president has the power to change national policy in favor of a foreign nation in return for foreign economic favors or benefits—so it would be odd if the framers intended the president to be exempt without saying so explicitly. See Olivia B. Waxman, "What Is an Emolument? Donald Trump Has People Talking About This Part of the Constitution," *Time*, November 22, 2016.

rants that claimed their economic interests were directly prejudiced by Trump's continued ownership of the DC Trump International Hotel and restaurant.[29] The second was filed in June by the attorneys general of Maryland and the District of Columbia, contending that the Trump International Hotel competed against Maryland's and the District's convention business while violating the emoluments clause of the Constitution.[30]

The third suit was filed in June by 196 Democratic members of Congress. They assert that their constitutional role as provided in the foreign emoluments clause (where the "consent of Congress" is referenced before any foreign emolument may be accepted by a federal office holder) constitutes sufficient interest or "standing" to merit review of their suit by a federal court. Here are some of the factual allegations from the congressional suit that involve President Trump receiving foreign and domestic economic benefits[31]:

- Management fees and other fees paid to Trump properties by foreign governments or by entities controlled by foreign governments.
- Hotel accommodations, services, and goods purchased by foreign governments.
- For *The Apprentice*, continued payments from broadcasters owned by foreign governments.
- Trump International Hotel, Washington, DC, and leased from the General Services Administration (GSA) its BLT Prime restaurant (with President Trump personally standing to benefit economically from both) have served, and intentionally been marketed to serve, foreign diplomats and governments. For example, it was reported that Trump International Hotel officials pitched for business to approximately one hundred foreign diplomats, post-inauguration, including from Kuwait, Saudi Arabia, and Georgia.

- The major tenant in Trump Tower in New York City is the Industrial and Commercial Bank of China, a majority-owned Chinese government entity. Negotiations for renewal of the lease will occur while Trump is still president. Trump also receives monthly management and other fees from foreign-government tenants, including Saudi Arabia, India, Afghanistan, and Qatar.
- Possible use of presidential power for his own personal or his company's economic benefit. For example, for more than ten years China had rejected Trump company applications to license exclusive use of the Trump brand for properties in China. Appeals to China's highest courts had been unsuccessful prior to his election. After his election, Trump told the president of Taiwan that he might revisit the U.S. "One China" position, meaning he might consider recognizing Taiwan as an independent nation and not part of China. Then, after meeting with the Chinese president, Trump reaffirmed the "One China" policy. Five days later, China reversed its position and granted Trump companies the right to register the Trump trademark.

The suit's alleged domestic emoluments include:

- Conflict of interest and economic benefit from the lease by General Services Administration (GSA) to the Trump International Hotel. On December 8, 2016, before Trump took office, the deputy director took the position that once Trump was in office the Trump Organization would be in breach of the lease contract. One week later a contracting officer said that GSA took no position on the issue. In any event, unless his widely criticized steps to insulate himself from his investments were effective, President Trump was in effect acting as the lessor and the lessee—a classic conflict of interest—as well as receiving even more financial benefits beyond his salary.

190

- Supporting policies that directly economically benefit President Trump's Mar-a-Lago:
  - President Trump is seeking a $32 million historic-preservation tax credit for the club.
  - Receiving payments made by members and guests.
  - Doubling membership initiation fees doubled after Trump became president; State Department and the UK and Albanian embassies promoted Mar-a-Lago.
  - Using his position as president to promote Mar-a-Lago.
  - Increasing the cost of goods and services, such as dinner prices, after Trump became president.

If the president knew of steps he could take to reduce or eliminate apparent conflicts of interest, and chose not to do so, that is further evidence of intention to violate the public trust and fiduciary duties that could, if proved, justify impeachment and removal from office. The key is Trump's failure to take actions prior to his inauguration that would have removed the potential conflicts of interest. Three actions in particular stand out.

First and foremost, President Trump could resolve a great many concerns and suspicions about his potential and actual conflicts of interest (as well as concerns about motives for colluding with the Russians) by releasing his tax returns—at least for the last ten to twenty years—which include disclosures of business deals, transactions, and tax issues, foreign and domestic.[32]

Every president since Richard Nixon has released his tax returns—and Nixon released his even while they were under audit!—for public review. The very fact that President Trump has refused—expressly violating multiple promises that he would do so, without any conditions attached—raises serious suspicions that he has something to hide. Even more troubling is that the explanations he has offered for breaking his promises are either outright lies or intentionally misleading—and we have already discussed that lying to the American people on issues important to the national interest is an impeachable offense.

Certainly, any congressional impeachment investigation should start with a subpoena to the president personally to produce all his tax returns for the last ten to twenty years. Refusal to do so—defiance of a congressional subpoena under the constitutionally provided impeachment power exclusively possessed by Congress—in and of itself would constitute cause for impeachment and possible removal from office.

The second option urged upon the president by many constitutional and ethical experts and rejected by him is to put all his business assets, companies, and transactions in which he has any possible economic interest, direct or indirect, into a blind trust. In this situation, a trustee is in charge of all the assets, and the trustor (theoretically) has no knowledge of what is happening with his portfolio. Of course, President Trump knows what he owns, and much activity of the trust would be reported in the news. So it is hard to say how much "blindness" would be involved. Still, at least a partial blind trust would be a start.

Trump also could have taken advantage of a lesser and narrower option to minimize possible conflicts of interest. He could have simplified his portfolio by selling specific company stocks in favor of broad index funds and bonds. This also goes for private holdings of property and businesses. By simplifying or converting all holdings to cash, a politician hopes to remove any suggestion of favor toward a business, industry, or sector.

The question is: Why hasn't Trump done any or all of these things to avoid even the perception of potential personal conflicts and enrichment as a result of his presidency?

The reason cannot be that he needs more wealth. Nor can he be worried about his economic future or that of his family. What reasons are left? Indifference? Arrogance? Greed? The belief that the ordinary ethical rules that apply to everyone else don't apply to him?

These are not legal questions. They are character and ethical questions. He hasn't answered them. An impeachment investigative process will require him to do so.

## Invoking the Twenty-Fifth Amendment

The Constitution provides for another method for removal of a president other than impeachment under Article II, Section 4. And that is the use of Section 4 of the Twenty-Fifth Amendment to remove a president because of some type of physical or mental impairment such that the president is determined to be "unable to discharge the powers and duties of his office."* The amendment was passed by Congress on July 6, 1965, and ratified by more than two-thirds of the states on February 10, 1967.

It is more difficult to invoke the Twenty-Fifth Amendment to remove a president against his will than to use impeachment to do so.

---

* Section 4 of Amendment XXV reads, in full, as follows: "Whenever the Vice President *and* a *majority* of *either* the *principal officers* of the executive department or of such other body as Congress may *by law* provide, transmit to the President pro tempore of the Senate and the Speaker of the House of Representatives their written declaration that the President is unable to discharge the powers and duties of his office, the Vice President shall immediately assume the powers and duties of the office as Acting President.

"Thereafter, when the President transmits to the President pro tempore of the Senate and the Speaker of the House of Representatives his written declaration that *no inability exists*, he *shall resume the powers* and duties of his office unless the Vice President *and* a majority of either the principal officers of the executive department or of such other body as Congress may by law provide, transmit within four days to the President pro tempore of the Senate and the Speaker of the House of Representatives their written declaration that the President is unable to discharge the powers and duties of his office. Thereupon Congress shall decide the issue, assembling within forty-eight hours for that purpose if not in session. If the Congress, within twenty-one days after receipt of the latter written declaration, or, if Congress is not in session, within twenty-one days after Congress is required to assemble, determines by *two-thirds vote of both Houses* that the President is unable to discharge the powers and duties of his office, the Vice President shall continue to discharge the same as Acting President; otherwise, the President shall resume the powers and duties of his office" (emphasis added). See https://constitutioncenter.org/interactive-constitution/amendments/.

Impeachment allows for a majority of U.S. House members to vote for "impeachment" (likened to an indictment), and a two-thirds vote by the U.S. Senate to "convict" and force removal; whereas under the Twenty-Fifth Amendment, removing a president against his or her will requires a two-thirds vote by *both* the House *and* the Senate.*  Moreover, a president cannot be removed at all without the initial support of the vice president.†

### *Conduct or Actions Justifying Removal Under the Amendment*

The definition of what conduct or actions suffice to meet this standard of a president who is "unable to discharge the powers and duties of his office" was not provided by the drafters of Section 4 of the Twenty-Fifth Amendment—and intentionally so. This was no different from the decision of the framers not to define the vague terms "high Crimes and Misdemeanors" as a basis for presidential impeachment. The drafters of the amendment also recognized that contemporary political standards and judgments would determine the appropriate

---

* In practice, with a resisting president, the Twenty-Fifth Amendment as drafted could require *two separate* two-thirds votes by the House and the Senate. The first two-thirds vote by both houses will be necessary if the resisting president hears ahead of time about an adverse vote from his or her cabinet and blocks the vote by firing the entire cabinet or those voting to remove him. Then Congress would pass a law designating the alternative "body," a majority of which would then vote to remove the president. A resisting president would undoubtedly veto that law. And a two-thirds vote by both chambers would be necessary to override the veto. Then the alternative body would vote by majority to remove the president, and another two-thirds vote by both chambers would be required to effectuate the removal.

† Some misread the first sentence of Section 4 and believe that the Congress can designate a body to make the initial decision on inability to discharge without the support of the vice president. This is a result of ignoring the word "and" and reading the word "or" as providing for an alternative method to remove the president for inability to discharge even if the vice president is not supportive. But this is not correct. A careful reading shows that the support of the vice president is first required *and also* support of *either* a majority of the cabinet *or* a majority of an alternative body created by Congress by passing a law.

definition of "inability to discharge" fitting for the time and the facts at hand.

It is also a good guess that congressional drafters of the amendment recognized that forcing a president out of office by declaring him or her to be physically or mentally unfit (especially the latter) would be very difficult, personally and politically.

However, there is an alternative view—that invoking the Twenty-Fifth Amendment could be easier if it became an overwhelming bipartisan consensus that, because of the president's mental imbalance and impairment, our nation itself was in danger. In such an event, the inevitably slow and political process of using impeachment to remove a president might be a luxury the country could not afford. If Trump's behavior became so threatening to the American people, enough to overcome the vice president's inevitable loyalty to the man who selected him, then the Twenty-Fifth Amendment—even if a two-thirds vote was required twice due to a resisting Donald Trump—could be the better and more easily expedited course, conceivably accomplished from start to finish under the provisions of Section 4 within four or five weeks.

## The Case for Assessing President Trump's Mental Stability and Possible Use of the Twenty-Fifth Amendment

To make an appropriate assessment of using the extreme remedy of removal of the president for mental impairment, experts must first determine whether President Trump shows signs of recognizable mental disorders or impairments that could create risks to our constitutional liberties or our national security, or both.

The evidence to date is that he does.

Second, a bipartisan leadership group in the House and Senate—preferably a joint committee of both chambers—should examine whether President Trump's specific words, actions, and conduct in the first year of his presidency pose imminent risks to our constitutional system of government or to our national security, or both. The answer to date is maybe—but serious investigation is merited.

*The Mental Disorder of "Malignant Narcissism"*

In 1984, the psychiatrist Otto Kernberg described a severe form of narcissism called "malignant narcissism," with personality traits that, in combination, constitute a significant pathology and mental disorder. He found that, unlike ordinary narcissism, malignant narcissism was a "severe pathology." It was characterized by an "absence of conscience, a pathological grandiosity and quest for power, and a sadistic joy in cruelty."[33]

An article published at the end of January 2017, less than two weeks after Trump became president, summarized best, in the opinion of various psychologists and other experts, the eight major indicators of malignant narcissists[34]:

1. A sense of entitlement ("like a toddler who never learned he is not the center of the world and becomes enraged when others don't meet his [or her] immediate demands")

2. Lack of conscience and empathy ("You know the little voice inside your head that whispers to you that you might be doing something wrong? Malignant narcissists don't have that. They also lack the ability to empathize with others.")

3. A sadistic streak (They are "willing to inflict actual emotional and/or physical harm, or humiliation to another living creature, and even gain enjoyment from it.")

4. Egocentrism (They "talk about themselves incessantly, seek compliments nonstop, and basically behave as if the Earth orbits around them instead of around the sun" and become "annoyed or even enraged when others fail to see things their way.")

5. Grandiosity (They have "an unrealistic sense of superiority; they may see themselves as better than everyone else, thus viewing others with disdain or inferiority.")

6. Paranoia (They are "excessively suspicious without justification, and/or [believe] that others are plotting against him [or her], read far too much into everything people say, and are quick to criticize, but they are not open to criticism themselves.")

7. A manipulative nature ("They will attempt to confuse you, maybe even making you feel as if you're crazy. They distort the truth and may resort to lying if it serves their end.")

8. Project their bad behavior onto others ("For example, if [the malignant narcissist] stole something . . . then [he or she] calls you a thief. . . . In projection people become unwilling to see their own shortcomings but rather attribute them to someone else. . . . They know these shortcomings because they have them, but they won't admit them. Instead, they deflect and insist the rest of the world is actually guilty of what they're doing.")*[35]

Sound familiar?

Of course.

This is the Donald Trump that most people recognize. For every personality trait described among these eight, it is not difficult to recall Donald Trump acting exactly this way on multiple occasions. Even his core base supporters should agree that these traits are more than a

---

* F. Diane Barth quotes psychoanalyst Dan Shaw, author of the book *Traumatic Narcissism: Relational Systems of Subjugation*, who described "five telltale signs of a malignant narcissist," i.e., someone who:
  - "is infinitely entitled and grateful to no one";
  - "when telling the story of his life, he 'leaves out any trace of his own significant misdeeds and failures";
  - "never hesitates to lie for the purpose of self-aggrandizement";
  - "blames others for his own errors and failures"; and
  - "is erratic, thin-skinned, belligerent, and constantly engaged in attacking and belittling perceived enemies."

little reminiscent of Donald Trump. In fact, to these core supporters, many of these traits are why they voted for him.

However, establishing that Trump is not normal and his personality and character traits closely track those of a malignant narcissist is still an insufficient basis to try to remove him from office under the Twenty-Fifth Amendment. The bar must be much higher even to begin an investigation. The key question remains: Does President Trump have a mental disorder or impairment so severe as to threaten the nation in two fundamental respects—a clear and present danger to (1) constitutionally protected liberties and the rule of law; (2) the security of the American people?

Based on President Trump's specific words, conduct, and actions in the first nine months of his presidency, there is evidence that he has sufficient traits consistent with a malignant narcissist and those traits present those two risks to the republic. Thus, removal under the Twenty-Fifth Amendment should be seriously considered.

Let's examine some examples regarding each risk.

1. Threat to individual liberties and the rule of law under the Constitution:
   - On May 8, 2017, President Trump asked then FBI director Comey to pledge his personal loyalty during a federal criminal investigation involving possible collusion between President Trump's campaign and the Russian government. Comey demurred because he owed loyalty only to the Constitution. This is an instance of President Trump's excessive egocentrism—putting himself and his own ego over the rule of law, indicating Trump's malignant narcissism allows him to ignore that this is a nation of laws, not men.
   - On February 17, 2017, less than a month into his presidency, Trump tweeted probably the harshest attack on the nation's media of any American president in U.S. history. He didn't

just criticize the media, as almost every president has. He described the nation's media as the "enemy of the people." Here is the entire tweet: "The FAKE NEWS media (failing @nytimes, @CNN, @NBCNews and many more) is not my enemy. It is the enemy of the American people. SICK!" After swiftly deleting that tweet, he then reposted a similar one, deleting the word "SICK" and adding two other broadcast news networks—@ABC and @CBS.

As the *New York Times* reported, "The language that Mr. Trump deployed on Friday is more typically used by leaders to refer to hostile foreign governments or subversive organizations. It also echoed the language used by autocrats who seek to minimize dissent."[36] Trump's generalized attack on mainstream media as the "enemy" of the people is a serious threat to First Amendment principles. Trump fails to distinguish between disagreement and demonization, between criticism and challenging the patriotism of reporters and news organizations. This is dangerous for a president of the United States, especially one with fervent, angry followers known to use violence against media, with the encouragement, even the exhortation, of Trump.

• In the first month of his presidency, Trump attacked various federal judges using personal language, challenging their motives, such as when his executive order banning any immigration from seven Muslim countries was struck down as unconstitutional by several federal courts across the nation, from Oregon to Virginia to Hawaii. In early February, Trump's Supreme Court nominee and now Supreme Court Justice Neil Gorsuch called Trump attacks on federal judges "demoralizing" and "disheartening."[37]

On April 26, a widely respected San Francisco federal judge, William H. Orrick, issued an injunction barring a Trump executive order with the effect of withholding funds for any "sanctuary city" (in this case, San Francisco) that refused to cooperate with what the city government believed was illegal federal immigration enforcement actions. Trump attacked the judge for endangering public safety and disparaged him for being "unelected," the very status under our constitution that the framers intended to guarantee the independence of the judicial branch. The *Washington Post* quoted Charles Geyh, an Indiana University law professor with expertise in judicial conduct and ethics, expressing concern about Trump's "dangerous message" undermining our Constitution. The professor said Trump showed a "lack of understanding of the equal roles of the three branches of government, specifically of the judiciary's job to serve as a check on the executive branch."[38]

2. Threat to national security:

- August 2017: Trump's reckless threats of nuclear attack on North Korea. On Tuesday, August 8, President Trump—without any consultation with America's military leaders or his secretary of defense—declared that "North Korea best not make any more threats to the United States. They will be met with fire and fury like the world has never seen." He said that North Korea's young and erratic leader, Kim Jong-un, "has been very threatening beyond a normal state. They will be met with fire, fury, and frankly power the likes of which this world has never seen before."

   This was widely understood to be a threat to launch a preemptive nuclear attack on North Korea—*the first time in American history that any president has ever made such a public threat*. Harry Truman never announced publicly his use of the first and only atomic bombs ever used in history (on

Hiroshima and Nagasaki). John F. Kennedy never made such a threat during the 1962 Cuban missile crisis. And during some tense time periods in the Cold War during the two terms of President Reagan, such a threat was never made.

From all evidence, Trump decided on his own to make the threat of use of nuclear power, scaring the living daylights out of Americans and people around the world, especially the tens of millions of South Koreans and Japanese whose lives would immediately be in danger if North Korea launched a massive counterstrike on Seoul and Tokyo using artillery, rockets, and bombs.

Several days later, he added to his original statement, again without any apparent consultation. He said that, if anything, his words were not tough enough. And then he said—again apparently without any consultation with the joint chiefs—that the U.S. military was "locked and loaded" to attack North Korea. And everyone assumed "locked and loaded" meant U.S. nuclear tactical weapons were ready to be launched against North Korea preemptively. Then he went even further to frighten the world, if that was possible: He implied that he might launch a nuclear attack in response to only *threatening words by the North Korea leader.*

Here was the ultimate nightmare case of the malignant narcissist personalizing the entire matter as if it were a contest of wills and egos between himself and the North Korean leader who is half his age, appearing to forget what was at stake if he miscalculated.

In reaction to Trump's heated rhetoric threatening nuclear war, former conservative Republican New Hampshire senator Gordon Humphrey wrote a letter to the New Hampshire congressional delegation, asking them to support a House bill to establish the Oversight Commission on Presidential

Capacity to begin an investigation of possible removal of Trump under the Twenty-Fifth Amendment. "President Trump's threat to rain down 'fire and fury' on North Korea is like pouring gasoline on fire," Humphrey said in a statement. "It's crazy. Donald Trump is impaired by a seriously sick psyche. His sick mind and reckless conduct could consume the lives of millions. The threat of nuclear war is steeply on the rise."

- Revealed highly classified information to top officials of Russia.

Another instance of Trump's putting U.S. national security at risk because of his reckless, ego-driven narcissism occurred on May 10, 2017, one day after President Trump fired FBI director James Comey. As discussed at length earlier in this chapter, without apparent prior consultation with anyone in the Intelligence Community, his national security adviser, or the secretary of state, Trump hosted top officials of the Russian government in the Oval Office, including the foreign minister and the Russian ambassador to the United States (the latter known to be a top Russian spy in this country). U.S. media was barred from the meeting, but Russian media was allowed to come in after the meeting to take photographs, with no Secret Service supervision.

According to senior government officials, as reported by the *Washington Post*, Trump's disclosure to the Russians "jeopardized a critical source of intelligence on the Islamic State" and "had been provided by a U.S. partner through an intelligence-sharing arrangement considered so sensitive that details have been withheld from allies and tightly restricted even within the U.S. government." Moreover, because of the nature of the information President Trump told the Russians, it was obvious that the source of the information was Israel—a fact subsequently confirmed in various public reports. "This is code information," a U.S. official told the *Post*, using terminology that refers to one of the highest classification levels used by American spy agencies. Trump "revealed more information to the Russian ambassador than we have shared with our own allies." The source of the information, Israel, would therefore have reason to mistrust intelligence sharing with Trump and the United States in the future, clearly to the detriment of U.S. national security.

## Conclusion: Beyond Mental Disability, the Absence of Fundamental Human Values

Put aside whether Donald Trump appears to have a mental impairment that can be characterized as "malignant narcissism." What we call his personality pattern is not important. The only way the Twenty-Fifth Amendment could be invoked—considering the need under the wording of the amendment to obtain the support of Vice President Mike Pence, a man who if nothing else has shown blind loyalty to President Trump—will be if substantial majorities of the American people are genuinely fearful of or repulsed by Trump's personal characteristics.

Each day, each week, we have seen Donald Trump say and do things that frighten increasing numbers of Americans. His approval ratings in his first year are the lowest in the history of the presidency. By September 2017, he had shown significant deterioration in approval ratings in the heart of his Republican base—rural white men without college degrees. Given the experience in the first year of his presidency, it is likely that each week, sometimes each day, Trump will make statements or unilateral decisions that will strike fear into more and more Americans. At some point, one might expect, a critical mass of that fear will overcome Washington on both sides of the aisle, and Vice President Pence himself, not to mention a majority of the cabinet, may act to preserve America from a dire threat that they and the American people perceive if Donald Trump continues as president.

If and when we reach this point it will be a traumatic event for the American people.

I hope that this epilogue is not read as a definite recommendation that Donald Trump be impeached as president or that he lacks the mental stability and judgment to discharge his duties and powers as president. At times, the words used strongly suggest that impeachment and/or removal under the Twenty-Fifth Amendment are worth serious consideration once all the evidence is examined. I still remain presumptively opposed to removal unless it is a last resort. Yet President Trump has clearly not taken seriously his oath of office, which includes a commitment to being transparent and ethical, and acting as a fiduciary to the American people. Most important of all, as president, he should not be allowed to favor a hostile power over America or urge a foreign power to interfere in our democracy, even if it helps him get elected. And his conduct and decisions at times suggest a serious mental impairment.

Whether the evidence shows that President Trump or anyone in his family or campaign was involved in helping, coordinating, colluding with—whatever the word—the Russians remains to be seen. But one issue is not in dispute: America cannot allow a president to continue in office unless he states unequivocally that Russia interfered in our presidential election to help him, that he regards that interference as a hostile act on the borderline of an act of war, and that he favors continuing—indeed, increasing—economic sanctions and political and international sanctions against the Russian government for that meddling.

Whether to decide to impeach and remove President Trump cannot be clear until all the evidence is fully and fairly examined, giving Trump due process and the right to present his own evidence and rebuttal. But not to begin the process and conduct a bipartisan impeachment investigation, given the undisputed facts and conduct already on the public record, is not acceptable. The American people, who saw him achieve the highest office in an impaired election process, deserve no less.

# Afterword to the Paperback Edition

*The Unmaking of the President 2016* was published in February 2018, a little more than three months before former FBI director James Comey published his book, *A Higher Loyalty: Truth, Lies, and Leadership*. Comey completed his book tour having received mostly softball questions from mainstream media interviewers. This must have pleased Donald Trump, for these interviews helped confirm to his loyal base that Trump was right about the bias and anti-Trump hatred of the mainstream media and vindicated in his decision to fire Comey. The coverage also helped strengthen his strategy to nationalize the November 2018 midterm elections around the issue of impeachment. And thus, the interviews helped divert attention away from the fact of his illegitimate election, thanks to Comey's improper intervention. The fly in the ointment of that strategy, as we shall see, is someone named Robert Mueller, who won't be deterred and couldn't care less about political attacks. His focus will remain on one thing and one thing only: the facts.

*1. Comey's Big Lie About His October 28, 2016, History-Changing Letter*

As Comey's book tour proceeded, I watched with amazement as among all the interviewers in the mainstream media—in print, cable, morning and evening network news, you name it—not one interviewer asked

Comey why he lied about the reason he said he was "obligated" to send the history-changing October 28 letter to Congress.

I don't use the word "lie" easily. I didn't use it to describe Comey's behavior in the chapters of this book. After all, it means accusing Comey of not just being wrong or mistaken. It goes to his intent—an intentional misrepresentation of facts—an act of willful deceit.

Comey lied, I believe—knowingly misled and deceived—when he wrote in a memo to FBI employees on the evening of October 28, 2016, and subsequently repeated afterward many times and in his 2018 book tour interviews, that he had an "obligation" to disclose the new Clinton emails to Congress on October 28 because he had previously told Congress and the public that the Clinton email investigation was "closed." He framed his choice as "concealing"—misleading Congress and the public by not telling them about the discovery of Clinton's emails on Anthony Wiener's laptop—or "speaking"—i.e., sending his October 28 letter to Congress. Between those two options, Mr. Comey saw no choice but to uphold the integrity of the FBI (and his own) to speak and not to conceal. He had to keep his and the FBI's integrity with such a binary choice, of course—because, after all, to paraphrase Marc Antony speaking of the hypocritical Brutus in a different (but not so different) context: "For James Comey is an honorable man."

But Comey's statements in his October 28 memo and throughout his book tour that he faced only these two choices are belied by his own testimony on September 28, 2016, before the House Judiciary Committee. Here is the exact exchange with Rep. Lamar Smith (R-Texas), who, along with all the other Republicans on the committee, was critical of Comey's decision not to prosecute Clinton:

"My first question is this, would you reopen the Clinton investigation *if you discovered new information* that was both relevant and substantial?"

"It's hard for me to answer in the abstract," Comey replied. "We would certainly *look at* any new and substantial information." (Emphasis added.)

So, in fact, Comey never said he would disclose first and then look. He said the opposite: He would look first and then decide. He knew that, since this testimony was publicly reported many times after he sent his October 28 letter* and much repeated in the months after in 2017–18. The false choice between "speaking" and "concealing" was contradicted by his own congressional testimony on September 28. The true fact was that he told Congress there was another choice—to *look at* the new email information first.

That's right. "Look at" first before disclosing. A huge difference. A historically huge difference.

So why did Comey frame his choices in such an obviously false way? Why didn't he look first at the Clinton emails before deciding whether to publicly reopen a new investigation, which he knew could hurt her presidential chances considerably?

He's not pathological about lying, as is Donald Trump—knowing that he is lying and not caring. The best explanation is that he was so good at his "Lordy, Lordy" image of innocence and sanctimony that he thought he could get away with fudging the truth, and the book tour interviewers proved he was right.

So, what was the truth? Comey, I believe, just couldn't, wouldn't, step up to the line. To do so would have meant that the entire carefully crafted image of himself promoted so meticulously over the years—

---

* E.g., *Washington Post*, October 29, 2016, "FBI Director James Comey Under Fire for His Controversial Decision on the Clinton Email Inquiry," https://www.washingtonpost .com/world/national-security/fbi-director-james-b-comey-under-fire-for-his-controversial -decision-on-the-clinton-email-inquiry/2016/10/28/fbad009c-9d57-11e6-a0ed -ab0774c1eaa5_story.html?noredirect=on&utm_term=.642f73394144; *Vanity Fair*, March 2017, "The True Story of the Comey Letter Debacle," https://www.vanityfair.com /news/2017/02/james-comey-fbi-director-letter. (The *Washington Post* article incorrectly attributed this Comey "look at" quote to July 2016 testimony before the House Government Oversight and Reform Committee. In fact, this Comey testimony occurred on September 28, 2016, before the House Judiciary Committee, as noted in the *Vanity Fair* article and many other media outlets.)

Mr. Transparency, Mr. Integrity, Mr. "I Never Consider Politics Noble Prosecutor"—would have been shattered.

We should now have no doubt as to the true reason why he sent the letter. Comey gave a strong hint of the truth when he said during one of his interviews, apparently without understanding how revelatory it was, that when he wrote the letter he was certain that Donald Trump would never win the presidential election.

So there, I am confident, you have the key to the truth he was reticent to admit: Comey thought, since there was no chance that Trump could win, what the hell? Why not protect his political rear end with the congressional Republicans, throw them some red meat to immunize himself from their criticism after Hillary Clinton was elected president? Even if something new was found among the Clinton emails on Wiener's laptop, the chances the emails were appropriately marked as classified and still ignored by Clinton—the prerequisite (as Comey had correctly stated in his July nonprosecution finding) to any finding of criminal intent necessary to bring a criminal case—were close to zero. (Out of 33,000 Clinton emails reviewed by the FBI, Comey conceded at a July 7, 2016, congressional hearing that *none* had been appropriately marked as classified.) So why not write the letter to protect himself from postelection GOP critics?

In other words, Comey made the ultimate political decision that every politician understands: It's called CYA, or "Cover Your Ass." But he self-servingly called it a decision to "speak" rather than "conceal." But wait: Comey also knew that he had opened a criminal investigation in August 2016 of possible illegal collusion between Trump campaign officials and the Russian government, which the intelligence community knew by then had embarked on an active effort to interfere in the U.S. presidential election through cyber attacks, hacking, and disinformation via Facebook, to tilt the election to Trump over Clinton. Did the "apolitical" James Comey use the same standard and decide to "speak" rather than "conceal" the fact of this FBI investigation of the Russian meddling and the Trump campaign's (or Trump's own) complicity?

Oops. How to explain the disparate treatment between "speaking" in the case of Clinton's emails on Wiener's laptop—which he had never seen before he sent his letter—and "concealing" the Russian-Trump collusion investigation, then ongoing? Well, Comey said, this was different: It was about a sensitive counterintelligence investigation about the Russians meddling in our elections, not the email practices of one of the presidential candidates.

As a law school professor once said to me when I was straining to distinguish one harmful precedent from another helpful one: that is a "distinction without a difference."

During 2017 and up to and through the writing of his book, Comey knew, and we all knew, that had he looked at the Clinton/Wiener laptop emails first before informing Congress, he would have determined *within six days* that there was nothing new there. (We know this with certainty because that was the amount of time, between October 31 and November 5, that it took the FBI to obtain a warrant and review all of Clinton's emails on Wiener's laptop to determine just that.) Thus, Comey knew with certainty that had he looked first, he never would have written his October 28 letter. Ergo: Donald Trump would have lost the presidency to Hillary Clinton. Ergo: Comey's impulse for CYA political protection gave the country Donald Trump as president.

So, when asked for the reason he wrote the letter, I believe he lied. He just couldn't confront the truth that his ill-considered and improper October 28 letter was the decisive reason how America came to elect Donald Trump as president.

Then, in early June 2018, a final reckoning of James Comey's misconduct occurred when the inspector general of the Department of Justice issued a five-hundred-page report that confirmed everything already written in this book: James Comey violated policies and protocols when he held his July 5 press conference and sent his October 28 letter. The inspector general stated his unequivocal conclusion: James Comey doesn't get to decide which policies to follow and which to ignore. The IG called him "insubordinate"—an understatement, to say the least.

The revelation that Comey used a private email system, mixing FBI official business with personal messages, on his Gmail account stored on Google's private servers rather than the Justice Department server, added a spice of irony and a "you can't make this up" aspect to the IG's report. *Seriously?* I thought, when I first heard this juicy new fact. Mr. Transparency, Mr. Speak Not Conceal, forgot to tell us that he had a private email system while he was investigating Hillary Clinton for hers? Oh, some of his apologists said, but unlike Clinton, Comey's private emails on a server that could have been hacked did not contain classified information. *Oh really?* I wondered. How would we know—since Mr. Transparency never told us and kept it a secret until the IG's report? And of course, no interviewer during his book tour ever asked Mr. Comey about his email practices.

## 2. The Mainstream Media's Complicity

Why did the mainstream media let Comey get away with this false narrative?

I think the answer is obvious, indeed human, but don't take it from me. I am a biased longtime friend and supporter of Hillary Clinton and a lifelong partisan liberal Democrat. You can discount my opinion: That the mainstream media gave disproportionate coverage of Hillary Clinton's email practices as opposed to her policy positions and preferred to blame her loss to Trump on her campaign's mistakes rather than take responsibility for their own excessive coverage of the email issue that dominated her campaign from March 2015 to Election Day.

Instead of accepting my opinion, take a look at what the *Washington Post* editorial board wrote, with remarkable prescience, on September

8, 2016, about three months from Election Day, words I chose to begin my book with:

> Imagine how history would judge today's Americans if, looking back at this election, the record showed that voters empowered a dangerous man because of . . . a minor email scandal. There is no equivalence between Mrs. Clinton's wrongs and Mr. Trump's manifest unfitness for office.

Yet, reporters and pundits who interviewed Comey during his book tour were disinclined to press Comey to take responsibility for the election of Trump and thus draw attention to their own responsibility for excessive coverage of what the *Post* described as a "minor email scandal."

Then there was the fact that when asked whether he thought his letter contributed to the election of Trump, Comey said repeatedly, with undisguised pain in tone and body language, "I don't know." Why weren't there immediate tough follow-up questions, based on hard, undisputed data? "What do you mean you don't know? Have you seen the virtually immediate drop in Hillary Clinton's substantial leads in Pennsylvania, Michigan, and Wisconsin from the morning of October 28, before your letter hit the media? Do you recall the 24/7 headlines your fact-free letter created throughout the media—'New Hillary Clinton Emails Criminal Investigation'? Didn't you realize those headlines and the dramatic drop of Clinton in the polls couldn't be nullified by your announcing, quietly on Sunday morning, two days before the election, that the investigation had found nothing new at all? Didn't it occur to you that all you had to do was look first before you decided to ignore long-standing Justice Department policies by writing a letter that could have at least some effect on the election results?"

I am not aware of any interviewer who cited the detailed data contained in the definitive May 3, 2017, study by the highly respected

Nate Silver (and expanded upon in Chapter 8 of this book with many other sources of data) regarding the decisive post-Comey effects on the election results in these three and other key battleground states.

Why?

The obvious explanation, human and true, is that the mainstream media to this day prefers to blame Hillary Clinton's many mistakes and shortcomings as a candidate (which she acknowledged in her own book *What Happened*) rather than step up to the line and take responsibility, as the *Washington Post* suggested, for their overcoverage of a "minor email scandal" as a significant reason why the nation now has Donald Trump as president rather than Hillary Clinton. I have close friends at the *New York Times* who have written me and told me how angry they are with my criticisms of the *Times*' email coverage in my book, even though I still regard the paper as one of the world's greatest. Yet none of them mentioned any inaccuracy in my reporting on their coverage of the Hillary Clinton emails.

### 3. Trump's Likely Happiness with the Comey Book Tour Interviews

Ironically, there was one person in the viewing audience of Comey's mostly soft mainstream media's interviews who, one can reasonably assume, enjoyed them: Donald Trump.

Why? For two reasons. First, Trump loved being vindicated, especially to his loyal base, that, in fact, the mainstream media hated him and loved James Comey. And second, the last thing he wanted was any focus on the Comey letter as the decisive event eleven days out that delivered him the presidency, since this fact seriously threw into doubt the legitimacy of his election as president.

Trump and his strategists have decided to make impeachment the issue for the November 2018 elections to rev up and increase Trump Country turnout. That way, they can sidetrack the issue of the Comey letter and Trump's illegitimacy—plus the serious evidence of criminal obstruction of justice and possible complicity with Russia in helping Trump get elected. They know that their best argument against impeachment is that partisan Democrats want to use impeachment to achieve what they couldn't accomplish at the ballot box in November 2016. The decisive impact of Comey's letter undermines that argument of overturning a free and unimpaired democratic election. Certainly, given the Comey letter's decisive impact in the last eleven days, the election outcome was not an unimpaired reflection of the popular will.

So, Trump and all the president's men (and women) have tried to reframe the 2018 congressional midterm elections as an up-or-down vote on impeaching Donald Trump, which they have good reason to believe will rev up their base and increase turnout. In the late spring of 2018 they escalated their efforts to politicize the Mueller investigation by accusing the FBI falsely of inserting a "spy" into the Trump campaign organization, leading Trump to compare his plight to the corruption of Watergate, calling this FBI operation "Spygate."

But an "oops" moment occurred for Trump on this Spygate conspiracy theory. After a highly controversial briefing of congressional officials, first limited to Republicans and then to the bipartisan "gang of eight"* by senior DOJ and FBI officials, the highly partisan conservative Republican Rep. Trey Gowdy—the same Gowdy who spent millions of dollars and more than a year investigating Hillary Clinton on Benghazi and ending up in a political rabbit hole—openly contradicted Trump and declared there had been no spying and nothing improper done by the FBI.

Embarrassing to Trump and favorite lawyer–TV spinmeister Rudy Giuliani? Probably not. Both men seem beyond embarrassment. They know their base will accept anything they say—including lies that they know their base knows are lies. Giuliani openly admitted his purpose

---

* Comprised of the four Republican and Democratic leaders of the House and Senate Intelligence Committees and the four Democratic and Republican leaders of the Senate and the House.

was to appeal to the Trump base, undermine Mueller's credibility, and get ready for an impeachment battle.

## 4. *The Undeterred Silent Submarine*

There is one big problem with the Trump/Giuliani strategy of attacking the credibility of the FBI and Mueller. That problem is Robert Mueller.

Some in Trump's camp have claimed to be taking a page out of the book of the Clinton strategy of attacking the independent counsel Kenneth Starr as partisan, leading a partisan investigation. (I was a part of that effort, and in retrospect, I have my regrets about too many attacks on Starr's motives and not enough on his questionable judgment and inexperience.) But Bob Mueller is no Ken Starr. Mueller doesn't come out his front door each morning to get into his car, with a cup of coffee in hand, and smile, ready to answer a few questions from the awaiting throngs of reporters. Mueller's office isn't filled with leakers who made no secret to reporters of their hatred for Bill Clinton and their belief in his guilt.

No, it's not even close. Bob Mueller is no Ken Starr. He is, however, something else—more akin to a silent but deadly submarine. Soundless, moving underwater without anyone seeing or knowing what is going on inside the ship; the fuel and ammunition of that submarine are called facts. Facts, facts, facts.

So far, as of late June 2018, Mueller's team has already issued more than twenty indictments and obtained five guilty pleas to felonies from key officials, including Trump's former national security adviser Michael Flynn and a top Trump campaign official. All of this was done in a little over a year—compared to more than eight years of the Whitewater/Clinton investigation and two years of the GOP Rep. Trey Gowdy Benghazi investigation. Yet a national public opinion survey conducted in May 2018 showed that a substantial majority of the American people—59 percent—did not know that Mueller's investigation has already resulted in these guilty pleas and serious charges against people in Trump's inner circle. That ignorance won't last forever. Additional indictments and published facts will start to get through to the American people and cannot be rebutted by partisan Trump rhetoric or Spygate slogans. Facts are stubborn things. And that is all Mueller does: facts.

In 1973, Richard Nixon said, "One year of Watergate is enough." One year later, Nixon was forced to resign. Trump's attempt to shut down Mueller's investigation—"one year of Muller is enough"—will fail. Despite all of Trump's and Giuliani's and other Trump surrogates' rants and attacks and attempts to politicize the issue of the investigation, the silent and leakproof submarine called Mueller motors on . . . and the silence and absence of leaks is driving Donald Trump crazy.

## 5. The November 2018 Midterm Elections and Beyond

If Trump doesn't fire Mueller, the result inevitably will be that Mueller will emerge from his underwater investigation and announce indictments of "all the president's men" (and some women, perhaps). And he will likely send a report to Congress, providing substantial evidence that Donald Trump was aware of, if not actively complicit in, the criminal conspiracy of his campaign officials and perhaps family members working with the Russian government, directly or indirectly, to interfere in the 2016 presidential election in favor of Trump and had knowledge that the Russian government had engaged in criminal acts of hacking and computer crimes to accomplish their pro-Trump goals. (Indeed, Trump publicly encouraged the Russians to engage in such criminal conduct when he urged at public rallies that the Russians expose Hillary Clinton's alleged missing emails.) And, perhaps, he will produce even stronger evidence that Donald Trump was involved in a conspiracy to obstruct justice with the corrupt motive of impeding a criminal investigation of himself and abusing presidential powers and fundamental constitutional values and norms in doing so.

To date all signs suggest that, even before such a Mueller report to Congress, in the November 2018 elections the Democrats will ride the Blue Wave we have seen in the last year, especially replication of the enormous increased turnout of anti-Trump women, young people, and traditional Republican conservatives in suburban and exurban areas who elected Democrats in heavily Trump-supporting areas in the various special elections that have occurred in 2017 and 2018. Such a surge of anti-Trump voters will almost certainly outvote even a surge from anti-impeachment Trump voters. A Democratic House, with Democratic majorities controlling the House Judiciary Committee, subpoena powers, and an impeachment process, now appears most likely, though not yet certain.

However, make no mistake: Trump doesn't really care if the Democrats take over the House and launch an impeachment effort. His reaction will be higher levels of adrenaline and greater numbers of early morning frenetic tweets—all adding up to "Make my day . . . bring it on." It will be just another opportunity to say to his base: "I told you so." Trump also is comforted knowing there is virtually no chance that there can be a two-thirds vote to remove him in the U.S. Senate, even if there is a worst-case result in November 2018 and the Democrats capture the U.S. Senate by a small margin. That is, if there is no smoking gun evidence, akin to the Nixon tape proving that he conspired to get the CIA to try to kill the Watergate investigation and then lied about it. Even then, Trump would likely hang on unless there are a group of principled Senate Republicans, as there were in August 1974, led by "Mr. Conservative," Arizona senator Barry Goldwater, who went to the White House to tell Richard Nixon he must resign or be removed by greater than two-thirds vote by the U.S. Senate. If that is to happen, today's Senate Republicans will have to come to realize that they must do so not only to save their party, but also because our nation's fundamental constitutional principles and historic friendships with long-standing allies are seriously at risk. More likely that won't happen. So that leaves 2020 for Trump to survive and get reelected or to be humiliated and lose—or, given his excessive level of malignant narcissism, to avoid the humiliation and to decide not to run again, blaming it all on "The Swamp." Meaning, he can decide not to run again and look forward to playing golf, being a media celebrity, perhaps starting a new version of *The Apprentice*, and maybe even actually getting to build a Trump Tower in Moscow with his buddy Vladimir Putin cutting the ribbon.

Of course, I and most people were wrong about Trump not having a chance to win in 2016. We can be wrong again. But I cannot resist reminding everyone who says we all missed it and the polls were wrong in 2016. In fact, the polls were virtually dead on in predicting Hillary Clinton's nearly three million popular vote margin over Trump nationally. And they were virtually all correct in showing her in the lead in the key battleground states as of the morning of October 28, despite all her alleged mistakes, especially by significant margins in the three critical states of Pennsylvania, Michigan, and Wisconsin, and thus, the next president as of that morning, but for the alien intervention of James Comey.

Whether another October surprise occurs in 2020—if Trump wins the nomination—remains to be seen. Given that Donald Trump has offered strong proof that he was right when he said that he could shoot someone on Fifth Avenue in New York City and his hard-core base would still love him and vote for him, anything is possible. In mid-June 2018, that not-so-funny boast by Trump might be tested, even among his core base voters, at the widely televised scenes of children torn from their parents, a baby taken from her mother while nursing, thousands of children in detention, many literally in cages—all a direct result of Trump's policies. His outright lie that it was all the fault of congressional Democrats was so blatant, so shameful, that even some within his own administration and Republican congressional supporters could not summon up the ability to repeat and support this indisputable and vicious Trump lie. Then he was soon forced to reverse himself and stop the child-parent separations, i.e., he lied about his lie that only Congress could do that. Everyone knew the truth: Trump had callously used these innocent children to try to deter those seeking political asylum from crossing the borders and to coerce Democrats to support funding the Mexican wall that Trump had repeatedly stated would be paid for by Mexico.

The utter immorality and heartlessness of Trump's use of innocent children was repudiated even by his own wife and eloquently by former First Lady Laura Bush. Signs of loss of support among his core supporters could be seen by late June, even among previous lock-solid supporters in the Christian-right evangelical movement.

Thus, by late June, Trump still could not get above the low or mid-40s in approval ratings, nor win significant support among independents, women, and suburban conservative Republicans. These low approval ratings for this stage of the presidency, despite a strong economy and the lowest unemployment in many years, showed that even in the best of times Trump remained a minority president elected by illegitimate means. It is therefore doubtful that he can win in 2020. If such is reflected in most of the polls as the 2020 election approaches, as noted above, I am guessing he won't run at all. His vanity probably could not sustain such a humiliating defeat for a second term. There is a serious chance that historians will rank him as the worst president in U.S. history—way below even Republican James Buchanan, another one-term president whom most historians now rank at the bottom.

Stay tuned. The wheels of history are rolling.

# Acknowledgments

My special heartfelt thanks to my longtime literary agent and friend, Ron Goldfarb, for helping me in writing the book proposal and for inspiring me to focus on the major misjudgments of James Comey and mainstream media that cost Hillary Clinton the presidency. To my editor, Colin Harrison, literally without whom this book would not have been written. He knew how difficult a task it would be not just to write the book but to make it relevant months after the 2016 election was over. He took my calls patiently, steered me in the right direction, propped me up when I was losing heart and energy. And finally, most important, Colin took an often densely written manuscript, overly legalistic at times and duplicative, and trimmed it down and made it into what I hope some readers will find to be an interesting and informative narrative as well as an important contribution to history. My thanks also go to the whole Scribner team: Susan Moldow, Nan Graham, Roz Lippel, Brian Belfiglio, Sarah Goldberg (who rode herd on the manuscript at every phase), Katie Rizzo, Cynthia Merman, and Elisa Rivlin.

Thanks, too, to the many sources, named and unnamed, who helped me with vital information to tell this story, especially Brian Fallon, Secretary Clinton's campaign press secretary and now an incisive CNN analyst; Joel Benenson, who took the time to put all the polling data in perspective; and the multiple sources in the media, intelligence, legal, and law enforcement communities who wished to remain unnamed but helped me understand what happened and why in the emails media coverage, the Russian investigation, and the lead-up to the James Comey October 28 letter.

I owe special gratitude to my DC law partners in Davis Goldberg & Galper—Adam Goldberg and Josh Galper—for their support; to Eleanor McManus, our other partner and cofounder of the strategic media/crisis management firm Trident DMG; to Carolyn Atwell-Davis, Drew Halunen, and Matt Stone, for their research on impeachment precedents; to Eva Bandola, who was there to relieve the tension of writing the book by teaching me about baseball elementals at a memorable Washington Nationals game; to Victoria Batts, my assistant, who assembled research materials patiently and efficiently; and of course, and especially, to Maddie Melendez, who has suffered through the boredom of working with someone for over seventeen years (!) who never has any crises or mood swings.

To my four children—Jeremy, Joshua, Seth, and Marlo—for absorbing another intense period of Dad's life writing a book and for loving me and blessing me; and to my six grandchildren—Jake, Sydney, and Devon (from Marlo and David) and Zachary, Noah, and Gabriel (from Seth and Melissa)—who I don't think will read this book but will still tell me they love me.

And finally, to the person to whom this book is dedicated—my wife, Carolyn Atwell-Davis—not only because she is my best friend, partner, and wife of thirty-two years (how did she do it?), but because she did so much to help me write this book. Carolyn is a great lawyer, a truly talented writer, and a great critic of her husband's often verbose writing—and even though I argued with her sometimes, I usually ended up agreeing with her editorial suggestions.

# Notes

**Chapter 3:** The *Times* Gets It Wrong Again

1   For the September 2017 study by Harvard and MIT scholars titled "Partisanship, Propaganda, and Disinformation: Online Media and the 2016 U.S. Presidential Election," see http://nrs.harvard.edu/urn-3:HUL .InstRepos:33759251. For the *New York Times* article, see Jo Becker and Mike McIntire, "Cash Flowed to Clinton Foundation Amid Russian Uranium Deal," *New York Times*, April 23, 2015, https://www.nytimes.com/2015 /04/24/us/cash-flowed-to-clinton-foundation-as-russians-pressed-for -control-of-uranium-company.html.

**Chapter 4:** The FBI Criminal Investigation

1   Evan Halper, "Federal Investigators Want Justice Department Probe of Hillary Clinton Emails," *Los Angeles Times*, July 24, 2015.

2   Josh Gerstein, "Dem Lawmakers Raise Doubts on IGs' Clinton Email Review, *Politico*, March 10, 2016, http://www.politico.com/blogs/under -the-radar/2016/03/lawmakers-raise-doubts-on-igs-clinton-email -review-220580.

3   Karoun Demirjian, "State Department IG Slams Clinton Over Emails, Wrongly Declared Dead at the VA, Europe's Migrant Dead Unraveling, and Obama to Trump: Stop Scaring the World," *Washington Post*, May 26, 2016, https://www.washingtonpost.com/news/powerpost/wp/2016 /05/26/state-department-ig-slams-clinton-over-emails-wrongly-declared -dead-at-the-va-europes-migrant-deal-unraveling-and-obama-to-trump -stop-scaring-the-world/?utm_term=.462efb2b86eb.

**Chapter 6:** Giuliani in the Shadows?

1  Peter Elkind, "The Problems with the FBI's Email Investigation Went Well Beyond Comey," ProPublica, May 11, 2017.

2  https://en.wikipedia.org/wiki/Rudy_Giuliani.

3  www.youtube.com/watch?v=HooSM2MmHFc.

4  Rachael Revesz, "Rudy Giuliani Says He Was Picturing Hillary Clinton in 'Striped Jumpsuit' While She Was Mocking Him at Al Smith Dinner," *Independent*, October 25, 2016.

5  Eytan Avriel, "'King of Oil,'" *Haaretz*, November 25, 2016.

6  "Comey Breaks Silence: White House Tried to Force Incapacitated Ashcroft to Back Spying Program," *ThinkProgress*, May 15, 2007.

7  Bethany McLean, "The True Story of the Comey Letter Debacle," *Vanity Fair*, February 2017. Two other postelection detailed reports about Comey, including why he chose to write his October 28 letter but, apparently with some inconsistency, chose not to publicize his knowledge that the Russians were meddling and hacking in order to help Trump and harm Clinton, are must-reads: Matt Apuzzo, Michael S. Schmidt, Adam Goldman, and Eric Lichtblau, "Comey Tried to Shield the F.B.I. from Politics," *New York Times,* April 22, 2017; and Elkind, "The Problems with the FBI's Email Investigation."

8  McLean, "The True Story of the Comey Letter Debacle."

9  Robert M. Faris et al., "Partisanship, Propaganda, and Disinformation: Online Media and the 2016 U.S. Presidential Election," https://dash.harvard.edu/handle/1/33759251 (Berkman Klein Center for Internet & Society research paper).

10  Jo Becker and Mike McIntire, "Cash Flowed to Clinton Foundation Amid Russian Uranium Deal," *New York Times*, April 23, 2015, https://www.nytimes.com/2015/04/24/us/cash-flowed-to-clinton-foundation-as-russians-pressed-for-control-of-uranium-company.html.

11  Elkind, "The Problems with the FBI's Email Investigation."

12  Apuzzo et al., "Comey Tried to Shield the F.B.I."

13  Elkind, "The Problems with the FBI's Email Investigation."

14  Jack Jenkins, "Giuliani Reverses Claim That He Was Leaked Clinton Email Information from Active FBI Agents," *ThinkProgress*, November 5, 2016.

15  Matt Zapotosky, "Rudy Giuliani Is Claiming to Have Insider Knowledge. Does He Really?" *Washington Post*, November 4, 2016.

16  Josh Gerstein, "Comey 'Enthusiastic' About Bill Clinton Probe in 2001, FBI Memo Says," *Politico*, January 18, 2017.

17  Ibid.

18  Yochi Dreazen, "The Anti-Clinton Insurgency at the FBI, Explained," Vox, November 6, 2016.

**Chapter 7:** The Fallacy of the False Choice

1  Karoun Demirjian and Devlin Barrett, "How a Dubious Russian Document Influenced the FBI's Handling of the Clinton Probe," *Washington Post*, May 24, 2017.
2  Greg Miller, Ellen Nakashima, and Adam Entous, "Obama's Secret Struggle to Punish Russia for Putin's Election Assault," *Washington Post*, June 23, 2017, https://www.washingtonpost.com/graphics/2017/world/national-security/obama-putin-election-hacking/?utm_term=.56119e4348c8

**Chapter 8:** Comey's Letter Elects Donald Trump

1  Nate Silver, "The Comey Letter Probably Cost Clinton the Election," FiveThirtyEight, May 3, 2017.
2  Brad Fay, "Comey Letter Swung Election for Trump, Consumer Survey Suggests," *Huffington Post*, March 6, 2017.
3  Sam Wang, "The Comey Effect," Princeton Election Consortium, December 10, 2106, http://election.princeton.edu/2016/12/10/the-comey-effect/.
4  Dan Hopkins, "Voters Really Did Switch to Trump at the Last Minute," FiveThirtyEight, December 20, 2016.
5  Sean McElwee, Matt McDermott, and Will Vordan, "4 Pieces of Evidence Showing FBI Director James Comey Lost Clinton the Election," Vox, January 11, 2017.
6  Kevin Drum, "Let's Talk About Bubbles and James Comey," *Mother Jones*, April 22, 2017. Drum's series of posts about the Comey Effect costing Clinton the presidency, on the *Mother Jones* website after the 2016 election and into the spring of 2017, are must-reads.

**Epilogue:** It's Time for an Impeachment and Twenty-Fifth Amendment Investigation

1  James Madison, *Debates in the Federal Convention of 1787*, TeachingAmerican-History.org.
2  Peter Grier, "Richard Nixon's Resignation," *Christian Science Monitor*, August 7, 2014.
3  *Deschler's Precedents* (Washington, DC: GPO, 1994), vol. 3, chap. 14, p. 2186.

4 "Comparing the Impeachments of President Johnson and President Clinton," NBC Learn K–12; Adam Cohen, "An Impeachment Long Ago: Andrew Johnson's Saga," CNN.com, December 21, 1998.

5 *Deschler's Precedents*, vol. 3, chap. 14, p. 2187.

6 For example, Keith E. Whittington, "Bill Clinton Was No Andrew Johnson," *Pennsylvania Journal of Constitutional Law* 22 (2000): 422–65.

7 "House Impeaches Clinton," CNN.com, December 19, 1998.

8 Susan Low Bloch, "Assessing the Impeachment of President Bill Clinton from a Post 9/11 Perspective," Georgetown Public Law and Legal Theory Research Paper No. 12-165, 2006, pp. 2–3; Charles L. Black, Jr., *Impeachment: A Handbook* (New Haven: Yale University Press, 1974), pp. 1–2.

9 David E. Sanger, "Putin Ordered 'Influence Campaign' Aimed at U.S. Election, Report Says," *New York Times*, January 6, 2017.

10 Philip Allen Lacovara, "What Is Obstruction of Justice?" *Washington Post*, June 7, 2017.

11 Richard W. Painter and Norman L. Eisen, "The Criminal President?" *New York Times*, May 17, 2017.

12 Eugene Scott, "Trump Threatens Comey in Twitter Outburst," CNN.com, May 12, 2017.

13 Philip Rucker and Karoun Demirjian, "Trump Says He Has No 'Tapes' of Comey Conversations," *Washington Post*, June 22, 2017.

14 "Memorandum Regarding Standards for Impeachment," Office of the White House Counsel, October 2, 1998.

15 Glenn Kessler, Michelle Ye Hee Lee, and Meg Kelly, "President Trump's List of False and Misleading Claims Tops 1,000," *Washington Post*, August 22, 2017.

16 David E. Sanger and Matt Flegenheimer, "Congress Said to Prod Trump, Who Denies Russia Meddled, to Punish Moscow," *New York Times*, June 13, 2017.

17 Clark Mindock, "Vladimir Putin Ordered Russian Hackers to Help Elect Donald Trump," *Independent*, June 23, 2017.

18 Mark Moore, "Trump Says Russia, Maybe 'Other' Countries, Meddled in US Election," *New York Post*, July 6, 2017.

19 Daniel Chaitin, "James Clapper: 'No Evidence' to Support Trump's Suggestion That Foreign Actors Outside of Russia Meddled in Election," *Washington Examiner*, July 6, 2017.

20 Jo Becker, Adam Goldman, and Matt Apuzzo, "Russian Dirt on Clinton? 'I Love It,' Donald Trump Jr. Said," *New York Times*, July 11, 2017.

21 Peter Baker and Maggie Haberman, "Rancor at White House as Russia Story Refuses to Let the Page Turn," *New York Times*, July 13, 2017.

22 "Thomas Jefferson on Politics & Government," letter to Edward Carrington, 1787, https://famguardian.org/subjects/politics/thomasjefferson/jeff1600.htm.

23 James Madison, "Report on the Virginia Resolutions," January 20, 1800, *The Founders' Constitution*, Vol. 5, Amendment I, Document 24 (Chicago: University of Chicago Press, 1987).

24 David Nakamura, "Trump Appears to Promote Violence Against CNN with Tweet," *Washington Post*, July 2, 2017.

25 John Cassidy, "Why Did the White House Ignore Sally Yates's Warning About Michael Flynn?" *New Yorker*, May 9, 2017.

26 Julie Hirschfeld Davis, "Trump Bars U.S. Press, but Not Russia's, at Meeting with Russian Officials," *New York Times*, May 10, 2017.

27 Sarah Wildman, "Trump Gave the Russians Israeli Intelligence. That's a Uniquely Bad Country to Compromise," Vox, May 17, 2017.

28 Zephyr Teachout, "Trump's Foreign Business Ties May Violate the Constitution," *New York Times*, November 17, 2016.

29 "CREW Sues Trump over Emoluments," press release, Citizens for Responsibility and Ethics in Washington, January 22, 2017.

30 Aaron C. Davis, "D.C. and Maryland Sue President Trump, Alleging Breach of Constitutional Oath," *Washington Post*, June 12, 2017.

31 Cristina Alesci and Jill Disis, "196 Democrats Are Suing President Trump over Foreign Money," CNNMoney, June 14, 2017.

32 Jill Disis, "Presidential Tax Returns: It Started with Nixon. Will It End with Trump?" CNNMoney, January 26, 2017.

33 Robert Kuttner, "Impeachment or Impairment—the Inevitability of Trump's Removal," *American Prospect*, January 30, 2017, http://prospect.org/article/impeachment-or-impairment-inevitability-trump's-removal.

34 Brandi Neal, "8 Signs of Malignant Narcissism," *Bustle*, January 30, 2017, https://www.bustle.com/p/8-signs-of-malignant-narcissism-34154.

35 F. Diane Barth, "When a Malignant Narcissist Starts to Unravel," *Psychology Today*, August 21, 2016, https://www.psychologytoday.com/blog/the-couch/201608/when-malignant-narcissist-starts-unravel.

36 Michael M. Grynbaum, "Trump Calls the News Media the 'Enemy of the American People,'" *New York Times*, February 17, 2017, https://www.nytimes.com/2017/02/17/business/trump-calls-the-news-media-the-enemy-of-the-people.html.

37 Julie Hirschfeld Davis, "Supreme Court Nominee Calls Trump's Attacks on Judiciary 'Demoralizing,'" *New York Times*, February 8, 2017, https://www.nytimes.com/2017/02/08/us/politics/donald-trump-immigration-ban.html.

38 Kristine Phillips, "All the Times Trump Personally Attacked Judges—and Why His Tirades Are 'Worse Than Wrong,'" *Washington Post*, April 26, 2017, https://www.washingtonpost.com/news/the-fix/wp/2017/04/26 /all-the-times-trump-personally-attacked-judges-and-why-his-tirades-are -worse-than-wrong/?utm_term=.34072a2899c3.

# Index

229

# Index

# About the Author

**Lanny J. Davis** is a lawyer, crisis manager, consultant, author, and television commentator who counsels individuals, corporations, and others under scrutiny on crisis management and legal issues by developing legal, media, and governmental strategies that are designed to best produce successful results for his clients. His clients have included CEOs, world leaders, and both national and international companies.

During the Clinton administration, Lanny served as special counsel to the president and was a spokesperson for the president and the White House on matters concerning campaign finance investigations and other legal issues. In 2005, President George W. Bush appointed Lanny to serve on the five-member Privacy and Civil Liberties Oversight Board, created by Congress as part of the 2005 Intelligence Reform Act.

He graduated from Yale College, where he served as chairman of the *Yale Daily News*, and from Yale Law School, where he won the prestigious Thurman Arnold Moot Court prize and served on the *Yale Law Journal*.